CW00860166

1OO
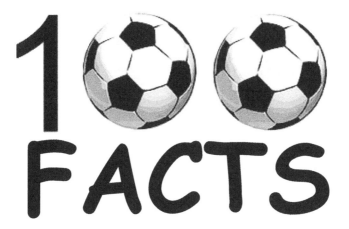

FACTS

Chelsea

First published in Great Britain in 2015
by Wymer Publishing
www.wymerpublishing.co.uk
Wymer Publishing is a trading name of Wymer (UK) Ltd

First edition. Copyright © 2013 Kristian Downer / Wymer Publishing.

ISBN 978-1-908724-11-3

Edited by John Kemp.

The Author hereby asserts his rights to be identified
as the author of this work in accordance with sections
77 to 78 of the Copyright, Designs & Patents Act 1988.

All rights reserved. No part of this publication may be
reproduced or transmitted in any form or by any means,
electronic or mechanical, including photocopying, or any
information storage and retrieval system, without written
permission from the publisher.

This publication is sold subject to the condition that it shall not,
by way of trade or otherwise, be lent, re-sold, hired out or
otherwise circulated without the publishers prior consent in any
form of binding or cover other than that in which it is published
and without a similar condition including this condition
being imposed on the subsequent purchaser.

Typeset by Wymer.
Printed and bound by Lightning Source.

A catalogue record for this book is available from the British Library.

Cover design by Wymer.
Sketches by Becky Welton. © 2014.

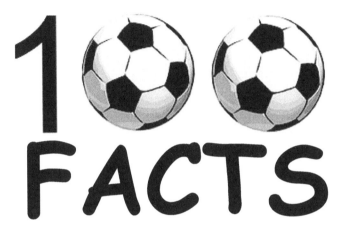

Chelsea

Kristian Downer

WP
WYMER
PUBLISHING
Bedford, England

STAMFORD BRIDGE ATHLETICS STADIUM

Stamford Bridge has been the home of Chelsea Football Club since the club's inception making Chelsea one of only a few to still play in its original stadium.

Stamford Bridge is a combination of the name of a stream near the Fulham Road and the bridge running over it. Unlike most football stadiums Stamford Bridge was not built for the football club that made it famous.

In fact Stamford Bridge was built long before Chelsea were founded having its official opening 28 years before the foundation of Chelsea Football Club.

During this time the stadium was used by the London Athletic club, with athletics one of many sporting activities hosted since its opening in 1877.

The origins of the football club lay in the vision of Henry Augustus Mears and his brother J.T Mears to create a super-stadium to host prestigious sporting events.

The ground was acquired by the Mears brothers who set about rebuilding it and contracting Archibald Leitch to design the new stadium. Leitch was an architect who was to become famous for designing some of the iconic British stadiums including Ibrox, Anfield, Twickenham and Highbury.

Designed to hold nearly 100,000 fans it was one of the largest stadiums in the country and would go on to host some important sporting events.

CHELSEA
FOOTBALL CLUB FOUNDED

Stamford Bridge almost became the home of Fulham Football Club a move that would have stopped the foundation of Chelsea.

After rebuilding Stamford Bridge, the owners needed a sports team to use it and the stadium was originally offered to Fulham to rent but they refused.

The brothers considered selling the land to the railways but during a meeting at the Rising Sun Public House (since renamed) they agreed to found a football club. So on 10 March 1905 Chelsea Football Club was founded.

This decision was the easy part; there was the small matter of recruiting the first players and finding a league to play in. The club initially applied to join the Southern League but objections from other London clubs led to this application being rejected.

The club went out and bought its first players and decided to apply to the Football League (a higher standard than the Southern League) putting together an application based on financial stability, a super-stadium under construction and a strong team.

At the time of applying the only club in London in the Football League was Woolwich Arsenal although they were soon joined by Chelsea Football Club who in May 1905 gained election to the Second Division of the Football League.

BUILDING THE INAUGURAL TEAM

The process of finding Chelsea's first team started soon after the club was founded in May 1905.

They started by appointing the clubs first manager John Tait Robertson. He was hired as a player manager from Glasgow Rangers. He contributed on and off the pitch playing 35 games and scoring 7 goals in the club's first season.

The club then set about putting together a competitive team buying three players from Small Heath (now known as Birmingham City) including future England international Jimmy Windridge.

The team played in a very different formation for today playing in a 2-3-5 pyramid with just two centre backs in defence, in the centre of midfield a left-half, centre-half and right half. Up front there would be five players in a triangle with the wingers on the far ends and a striker at the point.

The club's first match was played away against Stockport County in the Second Division of the Football League which ended in a 1-0 defeat.

The first game at Stamford Bridge saw John Tait Robertson lead by example scoring the club's first competitive goal in a triumphant 5-1 victory over Hull.

WILLIAM "FATTY" FOULKE
FIRST GOALKEEPER

FACT 4

Goalkeepers have a reputation for having different characteristics to other footballers due to the nature of the position, putting their players into the firing line.

Chelsea's first goalkeeper and biggest signing of the first season was William "Fatty" Foulke a player who was big in terms of his price tag, physicality and character.

The England international (one cap) cost £50, which was a huge sum for the time, but he was a big name signing. His size of 6ft 2 inches tall, and weighing in at over 23 stone certainly made him stand out. He was also known for his quirky personality and the size of his character more

than matched his frame.

One of the unique characteristics was that against the usual wisdom Foulke did not move to London after signing. Instead he remained in Sheffield, training with his old club and only travelling to London for matches.

Foulke was known for his size and was often called "fatty" by fans, however he seemed unhurt by this seemingly cruel name but was quoted as saying "I don't mind what they call me as long as they don't call me late for my lunch."

Foulke only played for Chelsea for one season making 35 appearances before moving on to Bradford City for the same price that he joined the club.

Despite his brief career, he will always be known as the club's first goalkeeper and one of the biggest characters in the club's history.

FIRST
BALL BOYS

Chelsea were the first team to use ball boys who are now a key part of the game, responsible for keeping the game moving by getting the ball back in play as quickly as possible.

In the past Stamford Bridge was quite wide and open with a large gap behind the goals between the pitch and the supporters on the terraces. This meant that ball boys would be kept busy, often chasing the ball great distances to keep the play moving.

Chelsea were innovators of this and used them for the first time in the second home game in their history against West Bromwich Albion on 23 September 1905. The boys were used to retrieve the ball when shots were made that went wide of goal.

It was reported that Chelsea hired their first ball boys to emphasise the size of charismatic goalkeeper William "Fatty" Foulke and intimidate the opposition.

One of the first ball boys was a 13 year old called James Ridley who lived a stone's throw from the ground. He was inspired by his time as a ball boy to join Vivian Woodward and other high profile footballers in the Seventeenth Middlesex Regiment during the First World War - the so called "Footballers Battalion".

The honour of introducing the first ball boys would not be the last time Chelsea were in the news relating to ball boys. In 2012 Eden Hazard was sent off for kicking the ball from under a ball boy who had laid on it to waste time during a League Cup game.

LONGEST
SERVING MANAGER

Recently Chelsea have not been known for keeping a manager for very long, changing managers ten times in the ten years between 2004 and 2013 but one of the club's earliest managers was also one of the longest serving.

After appointing David Calderhead as manager in 1907 he remained at the helm for more than two decades.

Calderhead earned the job whilst managing Lincoln who defeated Chelsea the season before which always helps get the attention of a club's board of directors.

Having been awarded the job he made a terrible start. It seemed unlikely that he would last a full season losing an incredible six of his first seven games in charge. Fortunately he turned things around and was able to guide the club to 13th in the table, which was enough to secure his job.

It did not seem likely at the time but Calderhead would go on to manage Chelsea for 26 years managing the club through a variety of ups and downs including the First World War.

Calderhead managed the club through two relegations although he was able to gain promotion although not always at the first attempt, taking six years to regain the club's status in the top division, the position the club was in when he left.

The main highlight of his time in charge was guiding the club to the FA Cup Final for the first time in 1915 which was the last one before competition was suspended due to the First World War.

The Scotsman left the club in 1933 handing over the reins to Leslie Knighton after an incredible 966 games in charge.

WHY CHELSEA
PLAY IN BLUE

Blue has always been the colour at Chelsea, with flags, songs and chants created to honour the club's colours.

The colour and shade however is not fixed and has fluctuated throughout history particularly in the last 40 years, when significant design changes have taken place every few years.

The decision to play in blue goes back to when the club was founded in 1905 and a light blue was selected in honour of the racing colours that the club president, Earl of Cadogan's horses wore.

These racing colours saw Chelsea Football Club originally play in light blue with the shirt remaining largely unchanged for many years. Eventually the shade of blue became darker and there have been many variations in shade, patterns and accompanying colours.

The home shirt has featured horizontal and vertical stripes in red as well as blue during various periods of the 1980's, however eventually the club have gone back to a more traditional blue.

During the 1994 FA Cup Final Chelsea played in "Royal Blue" however since then modern kits are much lighter and more reminiscent of the blue of the early years of the club.

FACT 8

GEORGE "GATLING GUN" HILSDON HONOURED WITH WEATHERVANE

One of the features of Stamford Bridge is a weather vane that forms part of the East Stand and has survived the redevelopment and modernisation of the ground.

The weather vane was erected in honour of George Hilsdon who played for the club in its second season staying for six years between 1906 and 1912.

Remarkably Hilsdon was signed on a free transfer from West Ham United and although he was a wide player, manager John Tait Robertson moved him to the centre forward role and the rest as they say was history.

Hilsdon was an instant success scoring five goals on his debut earning the nickname "Gatling Gun" due to his powerful shot. In his first season he scored 27 goals maintaining an impressive goals to games ratio of one every 1.5 games.

He was a trailblazer and the first Chelsea player to score 100 goals for the club. He went on to score 108 goals in just 164 games in a six-year spell. Such was his impact that he remains one of the club's top 10 highest goal scorers.

Another honour that he holds is that he was the first Chelsea player to play for England where he was just as prolific scoring 14 goals from just 8 appearances.

STAMFORD BRIDGE
FULL TO BURSTING

When the Mears brothers commissioned Archibald Leitch to build the stadium they had a vision of the ground being one of the greatest stadiums in the world.

Although the club was still in its infancy the crowds flocked to Stamford Bridge in ever growing numbers.

This popularity saw Chelsea continually set attendance records in the First and Second Divisions and even Britain, as football grew in popularity. In only their second season (1906-07) Chelsea had the highest average attendance in the Second Division averaging 18,425 fans per home game.

The popularity did not wane and by the 1919-20 season the average attendance had exceeded 40,000 with Chelsea again the first club to hit this landmark.

This continued in the 1930's with Stamford Bridge starting to reach capacity at home games. This was reflected by Chelsea having the biggest crowds for a single game in their division between 1929 and 1938. This includes the derby against Arsenal in the 1935-36 season, which at 82,905 remains the clubs highest league attendance.

Although limited by the size of Stamford Bridge in the modern era Chelsea continues to be one of the most attended grounds in the country.

By the end of the 2013 season it was estimated that over 40 million fans had passed through the Stamford Bridge turnstiles.

FACT 10
THE STRIKER WITH ONE EYE

The saying is that an "eye for goal" is an important part of being a good striker which made the signing of Bob Thompson from London club Croydon Common In 1911 quite remarkable.

What made this signing unusual was that Thompson only had one eye. However this disadvantage did not stop him from playing an important part in Chelsea's history. Thompson did not let the fact that he only had one eye affect his life or football career.

When asked how he managed when the ball went to his blind side he simply replied "I just shut the other eye and play from memory."

Thompson was one of the key players in the run to Chelsea's first FA Cup Final scoring six goals in eight games to help Chelsea reach the 1915 FA Cup Final. This final was the last before official competition was suspended due to the First World War.

Thompson continued to play for Chelsea during the First World War in unofficial campaigns where he scored plenty of goals.

During five "official" seasons he scored 25 goals with estimates that he scored more than 100 more goals for Chelsea during the unofficial games played during the First World War.

FIRST PLAYER TO
MAKE 300 APPEARANCES

Fans often remember long serving players that become part of the fabric of the club.

One of the first was Jack Harrow who spent 15 years at Stamford Bridge. Like Bob Thompson he joined from amateur London side Croydon Common in 1911 at the age of 23.

His time at the club was interrupted by the First World War that suspended normal games for four seasons but he was an ever present in the side.

His popularity and place in the side was attributed to his consistent performances that often saw him put his body on the line.

His long Chelsea career saw him make 333 appearances becoming the first player for the club to pass the 300 landmark. As a defender goals were not a big part of his game, scoring just five goals in his 333 appearances.

He finished playing at 37 but this was not the end of his association with the club. He went on to become a trainer and a coach, a role he kept until the arrival of a new manager in 1939.

FACT 12

THE FIRST OVERSEAS PLAYER

With the stars of the Premier League coming from every inhabited continent on the planet, it is hard to imagine a time when English football only featured players from the British Isles.

However for the first eight years of Chelsea's history they were represented by players from England, Scotland, Ireland or Wales only.

The pioneer that broke this record for Chelsea was Nils Middleboe a Danish amateur who joined the club in 1913.

The first overseas player to represent Chelsea almost didn't play for the club having originally signed for Newcastle. However he quickly changed his mind and was given permission by a director at Newcastle to make the switch to Stamford Bridge without playing for the Magpies.

An instant hit at Stamford Bridge he was instantly made captain and led the team out on his debut against Derby. A trailblazer at domestic level as well as international level he scored the first ever international goal for Denmark.

He represented Denmark at the 1908, 1912 and 1920 Olympics winning a silver medal in the first two tournaments, losing to future Chelsea teammate Vivian Woodward in both finals.

Middleboe played for Chelsea until the suspension of the league for the First World War and returned once hostilities ended, leaving the club to play amateur football in 1921. This saw him play for Corinthians and later Casuals FC before going into coaching in his native Denmark.

FACT 13   CHELSEA AVOID RELEGATION DUE TO WAR BREAKING OUT

In 1914 war broke out in Europe in what would escalate into the First World War.

The war would have an impact on every aspect of life including sports and entertainment such as football. After initially trying to continue the league with a view to boosting morale, as the scale of the conflict became clear it was decided that the 1914-15 season would be the last until the end of the war.

This final season saw Chelsea struggle in the league winning just eight games and at constant threat of relegation. This run saw the club fail to win and slump to a finish of nineteenth.

This was just one place and one point above rivals Tottenham Hotspur who had the unenviable honour of finishing bottom of the table. This meant Chelsea finished in one of the automatic relegation places.

However at the end of the season the Football League was suspended and when football returned at the end of the war a decision was made to increase the league from 20 to 22 teams.

The league gave Chelsea an invitation to remain in the top division giving the club a unique reprieve; the war had inadvertently prevented Chelsea from being relegated.

FACT 14   VIVIAN WOODWARD JOINS THE FOOTBALLER BATTALION

Few players make the transfer from Tottenham to Chelsea or vice versa, however Vivian Woodward was one of the first. An amateur player Woodward made the switch in 1909 going on to make over 100 appearances for Chelsea and scoring 30 goals.

Woodward's playing record does not tell the full story. He was a talented sportsman who competed for Great Britain at the 1908 (London) and 1912 (Stockholm) Olympics captaining the team to Gold in both tournaments.

Woodward's career was cut short by the First World War, playing just six games in the 1914-15 season because at the outbreak of war the government began calling upon the young men of the country to sign up for the army and Woodward answered the call.

Woodward joined the 17th Battalion of the Middlesex Regiment - a "Pals" battalion that constituted footballers from across the country including his former club Tottenham.

Whilst training Woodward came back to watch the final and was begged by his manager to play but insisted on Bob Thompson being allowed to play as he believed the players that brought the team to the final deserved to play.

During the war Woodward served with distinction rising from the rank of Lieutenant to Major and was injured on at least one occasion. His age and injury meant that he never played at the top level after leaving the army in 1919.

FACT 15

THE KHAKI
CUP FINAL

It took Chelsea 10 years from the club's first match to reach its first major final.

In 1915 in the midst of a terrible season on the pitch and the start of the First World War Dave Calderwood's men went on a winning run all the way to the FA Cup Final. This run saw Chelsea beat Swindon Town, Arsenal, Manchester City, Newcastle and Everton, a fixture that was played at Villa Park.

The run was overshadowed by the war with the game moved out of London to Manchester to ensure that the event did not disrupt the war effort.

It was held at Old Trafford in Manchester with a lower than usual FA Cup Final attendance due to the war. The game was dubbed the "Khaki Cup Final" due to the number of spectators who attended in military uniform on leave from service during the conflict.

Their opponents were Sheffield United and their sixth placed finish made Chelsea underdogs. Unfortunately Chelsea were overwhelmed and lost 3-0, a match where Chelsea failed to create more than a couple of chances.

This was Chelsea's last FA Cup Final for 52 years and it would not be until 1970 that they would lift the trophy for the first time.

WAR HERO FIRES
CHELSEA TO THIRD

In 1919 the Football League restarted following the end of the First World War and clubs set about rebuilding their squads after four years of war. In October Chelsea signed Jack Cock from Huddersfield.

Cock was a player with pedigree and was an England international recognised as strong, skilful with an eye for goal and an ethic for hard work.

This work ethic was legendary at the club at the time with the trainer was always trying to get him to reduce his workload, and even if Jack listened he would start up again as soon as the trainer's back was turned.

There could be no arguing with the results, he had an instant impact scoring twice on his debut against Bradford City on his way to scoring twenty-one league goals that would see Chelsea finish third - their highest league position in their history that would not be bettered until 1955.

In his other two seasons Cock was not as prolific but that did not stop him being the club's top league scorer in both seasons with 12 and 13 goals respectfully.

Like almost every able-bodied man of this generation he served in the Great War. Cock served with distinction rising through the ranks and earning medals and citations for bravery and gallantry.

At one point he was even listed as missing feared dead, but fortunately for his family and Chelsea fans he survived the war still physically fit enough to play professional football.

FACT 17

THE HIGH JUMPING GOAL SCORING KEEPER

Chelsea have had some eccentric goalkeepers in their time and Benjamin Howard Baker is part of this tradition.

He is the only goalkeeper that has scored for Chelsea. He was also a talented all round sportsman competing in the Olympics in the High Jump.

Benjamin Howard Baker signed for Chelsea in 1921 having previously played for a number of teams including the famous amateur side Corinthians.

A player that was an amateur for most of his career, he combined being an

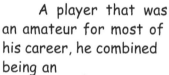

all round sportsman with helping his family run a hugely successful chemical manufacturing business, even storing some of the families products under Stamford Bridge.

Having represented Britain at the 1912 and 1920 Olympic games he once held the British High Jump record. During his football career he made two international appearances one of which was whilst at Chelsea.

He will be famous in Chelsea folklore for scoring in a competitive fixture against Bradford City on the 19 November 1921. With five minutes to go Chelsea were awarded a penalty and Howard Baker charged up the pitch to take the penalty powering the ball past the Bradford Goalkeeper.

Benjamin Howard Baker left Chelsea in 1926 and he remains the only goalkeeper to have scored for the club despite leaving Chelsea more than eight decades ago.

FACT 18

FA CUP FINALS
HELD AT STAMFORD BRIDGE

Stamford Bridge has had many uses in its life from its origins as an athletics stadium.

It has been used to host sports event at various parts of the clubs history such as Rugby Union, Cricket, American Football and even the Scottish Highland game of Shinty.

It has also been used for some surprising events such as motorbike Speedway and Greyhound racing that utilised the running track that ran around the outside of the pitch until the early 1990's.

The pinnacle of Stamford Bridge as a football venue would be the honour of hosting the FA Cup Final for three consecutive years between 1920 and 1922.

The first final was in 1920 attracting a crowd of around 50,000 fans watching Aston Villa lift the trophy. The second final featured London side Tottenham Hotspur which is likely to have been a contributory factor in a rise in the attendance to over 70,000. The London side did not disappoint lifting the trophy on the ground of their rivals something that would have frustrated Chelsea fans.

With Huddersfield and Preston contesting the last final at Stamford Bridge there were around 50,000 fans watching as Huddersfield lifted the trophy.
In a weird coincidence all three finals were settled by a 1-0 score line.

In 1923 Wembley Stadium opened, becoming the home of football and the permanent home of the FA Cup Final making Stamford Bridge the last ground in England to host the FA Cup Final, although the Millennium Stadium in Cardiff hosted the FA Cup Final between 2001 and 2006 whilst Wembley Stadium was being rebuilt.

MOST LEAGUE DRAWS
IN A SEASON

In 1923 Chelsea were almost drawn into the First Division relegation dogfight after going on a terrible run of 11 games without a victory that included seven defeats and four draws.

Towards the end of the season the club relied upon an incredible run of draws that helped them avoid the drop.

With two points awarded for a win and one for a draw at the time, these were invaluable in climbing the table.

The run saw Chelsea end the season with seven draws and a solitary win sandwiched in the middle of the final 8 games with the win coming at Stamford Bridge against Bolton Wanderers.

This run started with a staggering event that included three 1-1 draws in a row against Aston Villa and Manchester City at Stamford Bridge and away at Bolton. The final game of the season was predictably a draw with a 1-1 draw against

These seven draws were part of a season that included 18 league draws which is a club record but five short of the league record of 23 held by Norwich.

A STADIUM FIT
FOR A KING

Stamford Bridge has hosted many celebrities and dignitaries over the course of its history.

In the 1960's and early 70's it was common to see models and rock stars at the Bridge as Chelsea were playing the attractive and successful football that made them very fashionable.

However possibly the most famous and powerful was King George V who attended Stamford Bridge on numerous occasions as a spectator and in an official capacity at the FA Cup Finals held at the Bridge in the early 1920's. One high profile match he attended was an FA Cup match against Leicester in 1920 although this was not his only visit. He also attended some non-football events that included a baseball match in 1914.

Proof that King George V was fond of the stadium could be found in the fact that during his reign a marathon event was held that started at his residence in Windsor Castle and ended with a lap of the Stamford Bridge running track.

In the modern era Stamford Bridge still welcomes high profile guests enjoying the fine dining and hospitality of the corporate hospitality offered before and after every match.

OFFSIDE RULE CHANGE BENEFITS CHELSEA

In 1925 the Football Association changed the offside rule with the intent to increase the number of players that had to be between the player and the goal from three to the now standard two.

The new rules were quite drastic and teams spent the whole of the summer pre-season period adapting. Chelsea were one of the most effective at adapting to the new rules giving the club a fantastic start to the season. Chelsea won their first three games of the season scoring 13 goals and conceding just one.

It took time for the rest of the league to catch up and Chelsea would go unbeaten for the first fourteen games of the season in a run that included nine victories and some thumping results such as a 6-0 victory over Port Vale and 5-0 victory over Preston North End at Stamford Bridge.

Slowly the rest of the league caught up and Chelsea were not able to maintain their brilliant start of the season form, narrowly missing out on promotion.

The run however was impressive and fourteen games unbeaten at the start of a season remains a club record, although it was equalled in the 2014-15 season.

GEORGE MILLS
JOINS THE 100 CLUB

George Mills joined Chelsea in 1929 from amateur football and was at the club when Chelsea were signing the biggest name strikers in the country.

Despite the competition he was a prolific striker who topped the club's scoring charts on three separate seasons in the 1930's including his first season at the club.

During this promotion campaign he scored 14 goals from just 20 league appearances in what would be the last time Chelsea played in the Second Division for over three decades.

Mills star status did not last as he was overshadowed by the arrival of big name strikers considered more glamorous such as Hughie Gallacher however he did not become disillusioned outlasting these big names and still playing/scoring regularly.

He was at his peak during the 1936-1937 season where he was the top league goal scorer with 22 goals.

Mills finished his Chelsea playing career in the middle of the Second World War in 1943 becoming a coach for the club. He finished having scored 125 goals for Chelsea that puts him eight in the list of top Chelsea goal scorers.

FACT 23

FIRST SUPERSTAR SIGNS FOR CHELSEA

Chelsea have had a host of world famous superstars since the start of the Premier League and a reputation for signing famous strikers.

This trend goes back a long time and it can be traced back to Hughie Gallagher in the 1930s.

Signed in 1930 Gallacher was a superstar signed from Newcastle United in part of a spending spree by manager David Calderhead that saw three big money Scotsmen join the club.

This move was a massive coup for Chelsea as the Scottish international was a star of the game and a true character and always in the news, although sometimes hit the headlines for his contempt for authority and maverick tendencies.

Gallacher was sold to Chelsea whilst playing in Scotland's first ever game outside of Britain which saw him star on the pitch and get reprimanded off it for breaking a curfew.

Fate saw his second game for Chelsea as a trip to St James Park where a record 68,386 fans packed into St James Park to say goodbye to their former hero who is the most prolific goal scorer in their history with 143 goals from just 174 games.

Upon arriving at Chelsea he was just as prolific becoming the club's top scorer in each of his four seasons at the club with a record of 81 goals in just 144 games.

Despite his goal scoring heroics Gallacher was known for his volatile nature and indiscipline which played a part in him leaving the club in 1934 to join Derby County.

SEMI FINAL IS THE CLOSEST SCOTTISH STRIKER CAME TO GLORY

In the 1930's Chelsea spent a fortune on a new attacking line and expectations were sky high however the closest Chelsea would come to silverware was the FA Cup, reaching the Semi-Final in 1932.

This run started nervously with a draw away at Tranmere Rovers after a replay at Stamford Bridge that was an epic 5-3 battle. This was one of two ties that went to a replay with the fifth round tie against Sheffield Wednesday also requiring a replay at Stamford Bridge to take the spoils.

There were two high profile results with Chelsea beating local rivals West Ham 3-1 at Stamford Bridge. However the most impressive result was arguably a 2-0 victory over Liverpool away at Anfield.

The Semi-Final was played at a neutral venue in Huddersfield and the tie was given an extra story as Hughie Gallacher would face his former team Newcastle where he was still adored by the fans.

Gallacher would get on the score sheet but he was unable to power his new club to victory as Chelsea lost 2-1 and Newcastle went on to win the final against Arsenal by the same score.

This defeat would be the closest that Chelsea would come to winning a major trophy in more than two decades as the club battled to stay in the top division on a regular basis rather than challenging for honours.

RECORD
ATTENDANCE

Stamford Bridge was originally intended to hold around 100,000 people. However the closest that Chelsea would come to testing this capacity was when the dominant force of the time came to visit on the 12 October 1935.

The opposition were the reigning English champions of the time and local rivals Arsenal.

Records show that 82,905 fans squeezed into Stamford Bridge to watch an enthralling 1-1 draw which saw Chelsea equalise after Arsenal had taken the lead.

This record was set when fans used to stand for the whole match in tightly packed terraces, however due to safety concerns in the wake of a disaster involving Liverpool fans at Hillsborough, terracing has now been legally forbidden in the Premier League.

Nowadays Stamford Bridge like all Premier League football grounds is all-seater with a capacity limited to 41,837. This means that this record is unlikely to ever be beaten.

LACK OF SUCCESS
MADE INTO A SONG

In the early 1930's Chelsea had yet to win a major domestic trophy.

With a reputation for spending big money without winning a trophy and with its central London location close to the popular entertainment scene the club was often the subject of jokes from comedians.

In this era a common form of entertainment was to see a show at the music hall and one performer at such a show wrote and performed a song about Chelsea Football Club.

Called 'On the day that Chelsea Won The Cup' the song was about a dream about what would happen on such a day. Although the song does not say which cup, it most likely referred to the FA Cup.

The song works on the idea that a Chelsea trophy was so improbable that "the universe went off the real". The song has 12 verses each cataloguing unexpected topsy-turvy events that might happen "On the day that Chelsea Won The Cup."

It would be nearly twenty years from when this song was popular for Chelsea to live up to expectations and win a trophy.

FACT 27
WORLD WAR II
INTERRUPTS FOOTBALL

In 1939 war seemed inevitable and started to affect football even before the peace was broken. Clubs stopped making transfers due to the uncertainty that faced the world that summer. In September war was formally declared and formal competition was suspended as the nation mobilised for war.

The Football League was suspended but football still continued on a regional basis with Chelsea competing in the Football League South.

London was at the heart of the war effort, full of soldiers and diplomats from across the world, and football was a brief respite from the risk of bombing and the plight of the war.

Given the transport restrictions and limited mobilisation, attendances were small but with so many men around London it meant Chelsea could borrow some of the best players of the day stationed nearby.

Players to turn out for Chelsea as guests included future England manager Walter Winterbottom and Sir Matt Busby who would achieve legendary status at Manchester United as both a player and a manager.

War continued to rage until 1945 after which normal football could resume.

STAMFORD BRIDGE BOMBED

During the Second World War London was on the frontline, the country overcame the threat of invasion but suffered death and destruction inflicted during the Blitz.

The Blitz was the name given for a period of intense bombing by the German Luftwaffe on towns and cities in Britain. London was the capital and most densely populated part of the country meaning it was regularly targeted by bombers on both civilian and military targets.

Although Stamford Bridge was not a military target with its central London location it like the rest of the civilian population of London was at the mercy of the indiscriminate bombing from the Luftwaffe.

During games a huge flak balloon flew over the stadium to try and stop the bombers from interrupting the action.

Despite precautions two bombs landed on Stamford Bridge during the war, one falling on the West Terrace and one on the North Stand. With the North Stand under construction the damage was barely noticeable and easily repairable and neither bomb significantly damaged the stadium.

Compared to other parts of the city fortunately Stamford Bridge was not badly affected with no permanent damage or loss of life.

FACT 29
CHELSEA WIN A
WARTIME TROPHY

Football continued during the Second World War with regional leagues and tournaments set up to keep the public entertained.

Chelsea competed in the Football League South competitions and were able to call upon a whole host of guest players in London on leave.

Although not considered as important historically, Chelsea did have some success reaching their first competition final since 1915.

Chelsea qualified for the Football League South Wartime Trophy Final in 1945 where they played local rivals Millwall. With the threat to London receding, more than 90,000 fans packed into Wembley to watch Chelsea win 2-0 thanks to goals form George Wardle and John Macdonald.

The Second World War ended in September and the 1945-1946 season started in January with the FA Cup. Chelsea reached the third round before losing to Aston Villa with the games being held over two legs to help boost the revenues of clubs after six years of War.

Chelsea fans would have to wait nearly a decade for their next taste of success.

THE DAY CHELSEA PLAYED IN RED

Red is not normally a colour that appeals to Chelsea fans, whilst some kits have featured some red, it has never been the dominant colour in the home kits as it is the colour of rivals such as Manchester United, Liverpool and Arsenal.

There has been one occasion when Chelsea have broken with tradition. At the end of the Second World War Russian side Dynamo Moscow toured England to extend goodwill between wartime allies, Stamford Bridge was the first stop.

The game sold out and when the gates closed there was still 20,000 fans determined to get in. Some broke down doors, climbed over walls and snuck through gaps through fences to see this world famous event.

There was no official attendance that would do justice to how many fans made it in without a ticket, but it is estimated that up to 100,000 fans squeezed into Stamford Bridge on that day.

To mark the occasion Chelsea surprised everyone by wearing Red. The game itself was a cracker with Dynamo dominating the game for large periods but Chelsea took a two goal lead and the Chelsea Chairman was petrified that a resounding Chelsea win would spark a diplomatic incident. However he should not have worried, Dynamo grabbed one goal back before half time and dominated a second half as Chelsea tired, getting an equaliser but failing to deliver a knockout punch.

The game was a success but a situational one off in both the type of match and colour of the shirts that Chelsea wore.

PROLIFIC LAWTON'S BRIEF STOP AT STAMFORD BRIDGE

The Second World War affected the career of many talented footballers including England international Tommy Lawton.

A prolific goal scorer for Everton before the war he scored 34 league goals to help the Everton team win the League in the last season before the war. He was also an England international setting a joint record for scoring in six consecutive internationals.

When war broke out he joined the army becoming a physical training instructor, playing for Everton and making guest appearances for other clubs when he got the chance.

When the war ended he joined Chelsea for a huge fee of £11,500 making his debut in the famous friendly against Dynamo Moscow at Stamford Bridge scoring in a pulsating 3-3 draw.

Lawton was a fantastic talent and despite reports that he was past his best he was still a prolific goal scorer for Chelsea.

In his first full season at the club Tommy Lawton scored 26 goals in just 34 games, the highlight being a hat trick against Huddersfield.

Unfortunately Lawton and manager Billy Birrell did not see eye to eye and less than two years after joining the club he pulled off a surprise move by dropping down two divisions to play for to Notts County signing for a fee of £20,000.

FACT 32
BILLY BIRRELL BUILDS A FOOTBALL FACTORY

When Billy Birrell joined Chelsea in 1939 the club had a reputation for buying in talented players rather than creating them through the ranks.

After the Second World War Birrell decided that he would change this by creating a youth scheme that would develop players suitable for the first team in what was coined a "football factory".

With the backing of owner Joe Mears he set up a network of scouts and coaches at youth level including former Chelsea striker Jimmy Thomson as head scout.

The system took time to set up and flourish and Birrell was unable to guide Chelsea to any immediate success in the after war period. This eventually led to him leaving the club in 1952 before his efforts bore fruit.

He and his team had put in place the machinery for his factory and over the next twenty years a procession of talented youngsters rolled off the production line many of whom would go on to win trophies under other managers such as Ted Drake, Tommy Doherty and Dave Sexton.

Of the 1955 Championship winning team Ken Armstrong and Derek Saunders came through the youth system and a couple of years later Jimmy Greaves.

Of the team that challenged and won honours in the 1960's and 1970's the backbone of the side came through the youth team including Peter Bonetti, Ron Harris, Jimmy Greaves, Bobby Tambling, Alan Hudson, Ron Harris Bobby Tambling and Peter Osgood.

So whilst Birrell did not win trophies he left a legacy that would have a positive impact on the club for years to come.

MIRACULOUS ESCAPE ON GOAL AVERAGE

In April 1951 Chelsea were struggling in the First Division having failed to win in fourteen league games a run that included nine losses and needed a miracle to survive.

With just four games to go to the end of the season Chelsea were bottom of the table, six points or three wins (2 points for a win at the time) from safety.

From nowhere Chelsea found some form with a solitary Bobby Smith goal breaking the poor run of form in a 1-0 victory at Stamford Bridge over Liverpool.

In the next two games Wolves were beaten at Stamford Bridge whilst a Ken Armstrong brace at Craven Cottage gave Chelsea some hope going into the final game.

Things still looked bleak for Chelsea with Everton in the last safe spot two points clear of the Blues meaning that Chelsea needed to win against Bolton at Stamford Bridge and hope that Everton lost to have any chance of surviving.

Everton faced Sheffield Wednesday on the final day and they too could escape relegation if they won and Chelsea failed to win. It was the most dramatic of all relegation scraps, going down to the wire.

Chelsea won their game comfortably thanks to a brace each from Roy Bentley and Bobby Smith with the game wrapped up before half time and ending 4-0. This result relegated Sheffield Wednesday but it would be their result that would decide the Pensioners fate.

In the end Everton crumbled under the pressure as Wednesday romped to a six goal victory which meant all three clubs ended up level on points.

Survival would be decided on goal average, a

forerunner of goal difference which was calculated by taking the number of goals scored and dividing it by the number of goals that team conceded.

With an average of 0.815 Chelsea had the best average of the three meaning that they avoided relegation and Sheffield Wednesday and Everton would be playing in the Second Division the following season.

Chelsea had pulled off one of the greatest escapes in the history of the Football League.

END OF THE PENSIONERS

34

Chelsea Football Club were originally nicknamed "The Pensioners" due to a long and proud association with Royal Chelsea Hospital home to British war veterans.

The inpatients at this hospital are known as the "Chelsea Pensioners" and have been associated with the club since its foundation in 1905. So strong was the association that one of the club's earliest logos featured a former soldier.

However when former player Ted Drake took charge of the club in 1952 he felt that the association was old fashioned and not befitting of the club. This saw the Chelsea P e n s i o n e r disappear from the club logo and Chelsea became known as "The Blues" rather than "The Pensioners".

Despite the modernisation by Drake Chelsea have kept ties with the organisation proud of their connection with the countries armed forces. One of the iconic images on a match day remains the sight of "Chelsea Pensioners" in their traditional red uniforms sat proudly watching proceedings at Stamford Bridge.

On the game closest to Remembrance Sunday Chelsea like many clubs have a red poppy embroidered onto their shirts in respect to those who have given their lives to their lives for their country.

In 2005 when Chelsea won the league the Chelsea Pensioners famously formed a guard of honour as the players came onto the pitch.

PLAYING FOR CHELSEA IS
GOOD FOR YOUR HEALTH

In the 1950's some players believed that playing for Chelsea could be good for your health.

In the middle of the Twentieth Century many towns and cities in the North of England were heavily industrialised and suffered from a form of pollution called smog. Smog was caused by factory fumes and caused residents to suffer from lung and breathing problems.

Therefore in industrial areas it was not uncommon for doctors to encourage patients to move to where the air was cleaner, and compared to clubs such as Newcastle, West London was a cleaner place to live.

So whilst some players may have joined Chelsea due to the club's reputation, fame, or promised riches, there have been a few occasions when players have joined on the recommendation of their doctors.

This advice was to benefit Chelsea a few times with some iconic players in the clubs history moving to Chelsea to improve their health.

In 1948 Roy Bentley was one such player who cited his health as one of the reasons for joining the club. Bentley would go on to become one of the most respected players in the club's history.

ANOTHER
LAST DAY ESCAPE

FACT **36**

During the 1952-1953 for the second time in three seasons Chelsea were threatened with relegation to the Second Division.

Coming into the last few weeks of the season there were five teams battling it out to avoid the last relegation place. After losing in the penultimate game of the season to fellow strugglers Liverpool at Anfield there was a real possibility that Chelsea would be relegated.

Fortunately that same day relegation rivals Stoke City lost to relegated Derby County in their last match meaning that victory over Manchester City in their final game of the season would keep Chelsea in the First Division.

Manchester City themselves had struggled in the league but they saved themselves in their penultimate game, putting even more pressure on Chelsea.

This pivotal game was at Stamford Bridge with a nervous crowd waiting to see if Chelsea would survive. Chelsea started well taking the lead through a John Harris penalty and a Jim Lewis goal gave Chelsea a 2-1 lead at half time.

Survival was assured thanks to a Johnny McNichol goal after 62 minutes allowing Chelsea to wrap up a 3-1 victory.

This win saw Chelsea move above Manchester City in the table on goal average finishing in 19th place, just 1 point and 2 places above the relegation places.

Another great escape.

RECORD
DEFEAT

The worst defeat inflicted upon Chelsea was on the 26 September 1953 when the club made the trip to the Midlands to play Wolves.

Chelsea conceded eight goals with only Roy Bentley on target for the blues, a goal that was scant consolation in a humiliating 8-1 defeat.

Wolves played their home games at Molineux and were one of the strongest in the country and would go onto win the first league title in their history, winning by four points during a period when two points were awarded for a win and one for a draw.

The longest run of defeats came the season before when Chelsea lost seven games in a row between the 1 November 1952 and 20 December 1952. Chelsea under manager Ted Drake were rebuilding and eventually broke the sequence with a draw against Stoke.

Despite the European pedigree Chelsea have shown they have also had one or two poor results with Barcelona inflicting the two most painful results a 5-0 defeat in the Fairs Cup and a 5-1 defeat after extra time in a Champions League thriller.

CHELSEA WIN THE LEAGUE FOR THE FIRST TIME

1955 marked 50 years since the formation of Chelsea Football Club and the team celebrated in style by winning the Football League for the first time in the club's history.

Winning the Championship surprised everyone as Chelsea had not shown the qualities to be a contender having failed to finish higher than 8th in nearly a decade since the end of the Second World War.

The architect of the victory was Ted Drake the former Arsenal striker who was in his third season in charge of the club.

Chelsea were fired to the title by club captain Roy Bentley who scored 21 league goals. Success brought in the crowds as well and Chelsea averaged the highest attendances in England.

The championship swung towards Chelsea in early April as the blues secured a win over closest rivals Wolverhampton Wanderers, courtesy of a Peter Sillet penalty, which was the only goal of the game.

The magical moment and the title came with a game to spare and Chelsea were crowned Champions.

This was the club's first piece of silverware but the success was not to last, the next season saw Chelsea limp to 16th in the league in a feeble defence. It would be another 10 years before the club won another trophy and another half a century before Chelsea could proclaim themselves as the "Champions of England".

FORCED TO TURN DOWN THE EUROPEAN CUP

After winning the league in 1954-55 Chelsea were invited to take part in the inaugural European Cup that was created at the UEFA congress in March 1955.

The concept was for the champions of each European nation to play in a knockout competition that would crown the "Champion of Europe".

Chelsea originally accepted this offer and were drawn against Djuragardens of Sweden in the first round of a competition which was to become the pinnacle of European football watched by billions of people across the world.

The Football League's Management Committee did not believe that the European Cup would be successful or that it was in the best interests of the league for English teams to participate.

Alan Hardaker and his traditionalist values were key to the committee quickly deciding that Chelsea would not take part in the first European Cup.

Chelsea chairman Joe Mears was on the committee and responsible for the club accepting UEFA's invitation but he was unable to sway opinion and Chelsea did not participate.

The honour of being the first English team to play in the European Cup fell to Manchester United who refused to bow to the views of the league and it was forty-four years before Chelsea would eventually play in Europe's premier competition.

LONGEST
CUP TIE EVER

Originally FA Cup games were replayed until there was a winner once normal time with extra time had been played without a victor. That was until a limit was introduced by the government to reduce absenteeism caused by people attending football replays.

In January 1956 the reigning league champions were drawn against Burnley in the fourth round of the FA Cup. After the first game was drawn after Chelsea equalised they played the return at Stamford Bridge with Burnley taking their turn to score an equaliser as both games finished 1-1 with the replay seeing a goalless extra time period.

The sides met for the third time at neutral St Andrews in Birmingham with yet another tie this time Roy Bentley getting a second half equaliser for Chelsea as the fans enjoyed a goalless extra time scramble.

This meant a third replay this time at Highbury after Chelsea got to decide where to hold the game after winning a coin toss, this game was scoreless after two hours even though Chelsea game close a couple of times.

The final replay was at White Hart Lane and Chelsea finally won 2-0 and progressed to the next round.
Nowadays of course the game would be decided by penalties after the first replay so this feat will never be repeated.

This mammoth affair saw Chelsea play at five different grounds, in three different towns and cities, and in front of a total of 163,446 fans.

BOBBY TAMBLING
LONGSTANDING GOAL
SCORING RECORD HOLDER

Bobby Tambling signed for Chelsea in 1957 as a 15 year old schoolboy and was to be a part of one of the most exciting periods in Chelsea's history.

Tambling was a first team regular during the 1960's when a youthful Chelsea team were the fashionable club in London, supported by rock stars and actors. This fashionable exterior was backed up by results with the team playing with style and flair whilst challenging for trophies.

Tambling made his debut in 1959, making a goal scoring start to his first team career scoring in a 3-2 victory over local rivals West Ham United.

It was not until the 1960-61 season that he became a regular in the first team but once he had been given his chance he was prolific.

When Chelsea were relegated to the Second Division in 1962 he was made captain and rewarded the club with thirty seven goals in forty four appearances.

This form led him to be called up to the England squad where he was under utilised earning just three caps and scoring one goal.

Tambling scored in the FA Cup Final in 1967 but this was not enough to stop Chelsea feeling the pain of defeat against Tottenham. Although a member of the squad, Tambling did not feature in the FA Cup winning team of 1970 making just 7 appearances that season. This means that his only major honour was the League Cup in 1965.

He went on to feature in twelve seasons scoring 202 goals becoming Chelsea's all time leading goal scorer, a record that would be his for 43 years after he finished playing for Chelsea.

JIMMY GREAVES SCORES ON DEBUT ON WAY TO BEST GOALS TO GAMES RATIO

From the moment he was signed as a youth player in 1956 it was clear that Jimmy Greaves was a special player. He scored 114 goals at youth level, forcing his way into the first team at the age of seventeen.

On 24 August 1957 Greaves made his debut against Tottenham Hotspur at White Hart Lane scoring a second half equaliser. He then scored on his home debut as he announced his arrival with a bang.

Greaves quickly became the superstar of the Chelsea team scoring 22 league goals in his first season, 37 in his second, 30 in his third and 43 in his fourth and final season.

His goal scoring record had never been seen before at Stamford Bridge and is unlikely to again, Greaves scored thirteen hat-tricks and five in a game a ridiculous three times.

This contributed to him becoming the first player to score more than 40 league goals in a season in what turned out to be his final season for the Blues.

Despite his goals he did not win any silverware at Chelsea and he left having scored 132 goals in just 169 games making him one of the top ten highest Chelsea goal scorers of all time.

This also gave him a goals to games ratio of 0.78 goals per game which is the best for any striker at the club and is extremely unlikely to be beaten.

Reportedly against his wishes Greaves was sold in 1961 to Italian side Inter Milan. He only spent a few unhappy months there before returning to England when he joined Tottenham, continuing his amazing run of goals in the process.

If he had stayed at Chelsea it is difficult to imagine how he would not have far exceeded the current goals record held by Frank Lampard.

SELECTED TO REPRESENT
LONDON IN EUROPE

Stamford Bridge has seen some amazing nights in European competition including victories over some of the finest teams on the continent.

However the first taste that Chelsea got of European competition was more than fifty years ago in a competition called the "Inter Cities Fairs Cup" that was set up to promote business trade fairs.

The competition's validity has been questioned as the competition was not organised by UEFA and therefore many clubs do not list this trophy amongst their honours. However FIFA have subsequently recognised it as a major honour.

Chelsea were entered into the second competition which ran over more than one season from 1958-1960. In the first competition London like many cities sent a team made up of players from a collection of clubs in a city where a trade fair was held. However in 1958 London bucked this trend by sending Chelsea.

Chelsea's first game in Europe ended in victory with Chelsea travelling to Denmark to beat a Copenhagen XI 3-1. The second leg at Stamford Bridge also resulted in a Chelsea victory to secure a 7-2 aggregate win.

The Quarter Finals were played five months later which was unusual for most competitions but not the Fairs Cup. Chelsea started the tie well with a 1-0 home victory over a Belgrade XI. The trip to Yugoslavia was not as successful with the team from what is now Serbia running out 4-1 victors and eliminating Chelsea 4-2 on aggregate.

The competition was eventually won by Barcelona who defeated Birmingham City in March 1960 more than 17 months after the start of the competition.

TED DRAKE
REPLACED BY THE DOC

After nine seasons at Stamford Bridge manager Ted Drake left Chelsea early into the 1961/1962 campaign after an eventful time at the club.

He left having transformed the club introducing tougher ball based training, changing the recruitment process to rely less on unreliable big name signings and more on an extensive scouting network.

This tougher image extended to the fans encouraging them to get behind the team rather than cheering the football, he discarded the old-fashioned nickname and introduced a new crest featuring a lion.

This new mentality translated into success, surprising the establishment by winning the league in 1955. This was the high point of his tenure with Chelsea unable to maintain this success and the following seasons saw the club consistently mired in mid table mediocrity.

He left with having continued Billy Birrell's legacy of developing youth players. One of the high points of these later years was the emergence of Jimmy Greaves. Greaves may have been sold but he was just part of the production line with the backbone of the 1960's side that saw so much success benefitting from Ted Drake's work.

He was replaced by Chelsea player/coach Tommy Docherty who would after a relegation setback build on his work to turn Chelsea into a side chasing trophies once more.

PROMOTION ON
GOAL AVERAGE

Chelsea were relegated in 1962 and put together a strong campaign for promotion in their first full season under new manager Tommy Docherty, however not for the first time they would rely on "goal average" to help them out.

The Blues started the season strongly winning their first three games scoring nine goals without reply, this form tailed away slightly but six wins in a row saw them go thirteen games unbeaten which included 11 wins and a run of six wins in a row.

However in February the form nose-dived, losing five league games in a row although they recovered slightly but with three games to play Chelsea had dropped to third. With the second placed team having already played their 42 games Chelsea knew that a comfortable victory would be enough to secure promotion.

They faced Portsmouth at Stamford Bridge and took just two minutes to ease the nerves of the spectators with Derek Kevan opening the scoring in what was his only goal for the club.

Promotion was assured by half time with two Bobby Tambling goals to give Chelsea a 3-0 lead. Tambling completed his hat-trick soon after the restart, scoring four in total with Frank Blunstone and Terry Venables the other players on the score sheet as Chelsea finished up 7-0 winners.

It was sufficient to secure promotion by overtaking Sunderland on goal average.

BORN IS THE KING OF STAMFORD BRIDGE

In 1964 Peter Osgood forced his way into the Chelsea first team after scoring more than a goal a game for the reserves. He made his debut against Workington in the League Cup scoring two goals and the King of Stamford Bridge was born.

A centre forward he recovered from a broken leg early in his career to become Chelsea's star striker in the late 1960's and early 1970's as The Blues challenged for major honours winning the FA Cup and European Cup Winners Cup in successive seasons.

He left Chelsea in 1974 as the great team that came together in the late 1960's broke up following disagreements with Chelsea manager Dave Sexton about his lifestyle. When he was placed on the transfer list fans picketed the ground trying to get him to stay yet he was sold to Southampton where he played for four seasons.

After a spell on loan to Norwich and in the United States playing for Philadelphia Osgood returned to Chelsea in 1978 making a handful of appearances before finally retiring just over a year later.

Adored by Chelsea fans he had his own song that was still sung at Stamford Bridge decades after he stopped playing:

Out from the Shed came a rising Young star
scoring past Pat Jennings from near and from far
and the Chelsea won as we all knew they would.
The star of that team was Peter Osgood
Osgood Osgood Osgood Osgood
Born is the king of Stamford Bridge

Peter Osgood died suddenly in 2006 aged just 59 and his after a memorial service his ashes were laid to rest under the penalty spot in front of the Shed End at Stamford Bridge.

In 2010 a permanent tribute to Osgood was unveiled at Stamford Bridge with a statue outside the Millennium entrance.

FIRST
LEAGUE CUP

The first knockout competition that Chelsea won was the League Cup when they lifted the trophy in 1965 after beating Leicester City in a two-legged final, a format that has since been scrapped in favour of a one off showpiece final at Wembley Stadium.

On the way to the final Chelsea beat Birmingham City, Notts County, Swansea City, Workington Town and Aston Villa.

The first leg of the final was played at Stamford Bridge which Chelsea won 3-2 with Bobby Tambling, Terry Venables and Eddie McCreadie scoring the goals. Needing only a draw in the return leg they played out a goalless draw at Leicester's Filbert Street ground.

This was the club's first trophy in a decade and the first indication of the progress that Tommy Docherty was making moulding his promising youth talent into a team that could challenge for major honours.

WINNING BY THE
TOSS OF A COIN

Losing football matches is always difficult to take. However imagine losing one by the toss of a coin.

This is exactly what happened to Chelsea's opponents in the last 16 of the Inter Cities Fairs Cup in 1966.

Having played two legs that ended in stalemate and a play-off that ended 1-1 it was decided that with no option of a further replay and penalties not part of the format of the game at the time, the tie was decided by the toss of a coin.

The first leg was in Milan at the San Siro stadium. Chelsea lost 2-1 with George Graham scoring a last minute consolation to keep Chelsea in the tie.

In the return leg Chelsea scored two early goals with Graham joined on the score sheet by Peter Osgood and the Italians scoring just before half time and with no further goals the game went to a play off in Italy.

The play-off at the San Siro saw Chelsea take an early lead and hold it until the last minute of normal time before the Italians equalised. Chelsea then famously progressed to the quarter-finals courtesy of the toss of German referee Herr Baumgartner's Deutschmark.

FACT 49
HIGH SCORING DRAW AGAINST WORLD CUP STARS

The first game that England's World Cup heroes Bobby Moore, Martin Peters and Geoff Hurst played after lifting the trophy was against Chelsea at Upton Park and saw Chelsea's players applaud West Ham as they were presented to the crowd.

The exciting game of the season though was in the return fixture in December at Stamford Bridge that ended as a 10-goal thriller.

This game stands as the joint highest scoring draw in Chelsea history with the other game against Bolton in 1937.

The game in 1966 had it all Chelsea went 2-0 before scoring once before half time and then twice quickly after the start of the second half to take a 3-2 lead.

This comeback did not last long as West ham scored three goals in six minutes to take a 5-3 lead in what was a manic eleven minutes between the 51st and 61st minute that saw four goals scored.

In a game that had already swung both ways Chelsea again came charging back from a two goal deficit with two goals from Bobby Tambling that included a penalty with ten minutes to go and then a dramatic equaliser in injury time.

This was an incredible game that had it all with the teams duly sharing the points.

FIRST ALL LONDON
FA CUP FINAL

In 1967 Chelsea qualified for their second FA Cup Final more than half a century after the first.

The final was the first that Chelsea would play at Wembley and they faced familiar foe Tottenham Hotspur in what was the first FA Cup Final contested by two London clubs.

led the game to be nicknamed the "Cockney Cup Final" and there was an estimated crowd of 100,000 in the stadium to watch the action unfold.

Chelsea faced a Spurs side that featured two former players, the prolific Jimmy Greaves and former captain and future England manager Terry Venables.

The game saw Tottenham dominate and hold a two goal lead going into the last ten minutes, Chelsea did fight back in the closing stages with Bobby Tambling giving the Blues hope with five minutes remaining but Spurs held on to deny Chelsea their first FA Cup trophy.

Tottenham won the game but fortunately for Chelsea it would not be another fifty years before they reached their next final.

Of those on the field in 1967 only Allan Harris, Tony Hateley and Bobby Tambling not involved in the next one just three years later.

FIRST
51 PLAYER OF THE YEAR

Being voted for by the fans the Player of the Year award is the highest honour fans can give to a player.

The first player to receive this honour was goalkeeper Peter Bonetti. The award to a goalkeeper was to prove unusual with only three other goalkeepers earning the honour in the first 45 years of the award.

However as one of the stars of the team it was not surprising that the award went to Bonetti who was one of the stars of his generation at Chelsea.

Born just a few miles from Stamford Bridge he made his debut in 1960 and quickly became first choice goalkeeper a position he would hold for all but a season in the next 19 years.

Nicknamed "the cat" due to his quick reflexes Bonetti won seven England caps and was part of the World Cup winning England squad of 1966.

Although he made no appearances he was eventually awarded a winners medal in 2009 after a campaign to acknowledge those who did not appear in the finals but were in the squad.

Bonetti was one of Chelsea's most loyal and longest-serving players who went on to make 729 appearances in total.

IAN HUTCHINSON'S
52 WINDMILL LONG THROWS

In the Premier League Rory Delap sparked a trend for long throws however one of the first players to make a long throw his trademark was Ian Hutchinson who played for The Blues between 1968-1976.

A striker by trade he scored 48 goals in 148 appearances but will be remembered for his part in the

exciting team of the late 1960's and early 1970's as well as his devastating long throws.

His throws were often described as having a windmill like action. They proved an effective weapon allowing throw-ins inside the opposition half to be a real attacking opportunity almost like having a corner.

The most famous use of this weapon was in the FA Cup. In the 1970 FA Cup Final replay he launched a 40-yard throw in that David Webb headed home to allow Chelsea to lift the trophy.

He was able to add this assist to his vital equalising goal in his traditional position within the box with just minutes left in the original 1970 FA Cup Final.

Unfortunately Hutchinson was plagued by injuries that limited his appearances towards the end of his career and he was forced to retire before he reached 30.

THE
PHANTOM GOAL

A "phantom" or "ghost" goal is the name given for goals that are incorrectly awarded by the referee because they not cross the line. Regardless of evidence after the game these goals are counted in the game score and statistics.

There are some famous "phantom" or "ghost" goals with the most infamous against Chelsea being the one attributed to Liverpool's Luis Garcia in the Semi-Final of the Champions League in 2005 with Chelsea fans adamant to this day that the goal should not have stood.

However Chelsea have also benefited from "ghost" goals. The first instance was in 1970 when Alan Hudson took a shot from outside the area that struck the side netting and bounced out.

Hudson did not celebrate and the players set for a goal kick until referee Roy Capey awarded a goal to the surprise of the Chelsea players and disbelief of those playing and supporting Ipswich.

There is also the 2012 FA Cup Semi-Final where Juan Mata took a shot with a heap of bodies on the line after a goal mouth melee. The referee awarded a goal but replays showed the ball clearly did not cross the line. This was a key moment in the match but few Chelsea fans have ever complained about this refereeing decision.

With the advent of goal line technology in the Premier League such situations are unlikely to happen again.

THIRD TIME LUCKY
FACT 54 IN THE FA CUP

The first two times Chelsea made it to the FA Cup they fell at the final hurdle suffering defeat at the hands of Sheffield United (1915) and Tottenham Hotspur (1967).

1970 saw a flamboyant Chelsea side reach the final for the third time, with one of the top teams of the era Leeds United, standing between them and lifting the trophy for the first time.

The Final was played at Wembley and Chelsea equalised twice during the game the second time courtesy of an Ian Hutchinson header with just four minutes left to play. After 90 minutes the scores were level and as per the regulations at the time the game went to a replay that would be played at Old Trafford.

This was the first FA Cup Final replay since 1912 and the first time a final had been played outside of Wembley since it opened in 1923.

The Manchester replay was another tight and often vicious encounter between fierce rivals. Leeds took the lead in the first half and Chelsea trailed until 11 minutes from time when Peter Osgood equalised to send the game in to extra time.

Chelsea took the lead for the first time in the tie courtesy of a long throw from Ian Hutchinson that was converted by defender and future caretaker manager David Webb.

Chelsea did not surrender their lead and held on to secure their first FA Cup win.

55

PETER OSGOOD
SCORES IN EVERY ROUND

To win the FA Cup teams from the top divisions have to play six rounds before they can lift the trophy.

In the history of the competition only nine players have scored in every round of the FA Cup. The last player to achieve this feat was Peter Osgood in Chelsea's triumphant 1970 FA Cup run.

He did not score in every game but was on the score sheet at least once in every round.

Osgood started this phenomenal run with a first half goal in the third round at Stamford Bridge against Birmingham before getting one in the first game of a replayed tie against Burnley in the fourth round.

Osgood was then on the score sheet for the victorious fifth round tie against Crystal Palace before blowing away another London rival Queens Park Rangers with a stunning hat-trick in the quarter-final.

In the semi-final he scored the second goal in a five goal annihilation of Watford that set up a final against Leeds.

Osgood did not score in the Final at Wembley but in the replay he scored the late equaliser that sent the game to extra time completing his record of scoring in every round of the competition.

The only Chelsea player to have achieved this record, the only player to have come close was Gavin Peacock who scored in every round except the final in 1994, having hit the bar when the scores were 0-0 in a 4-0 defeat.

RECORD WIN

The record win scored by Chelsea was in the early rounds of the European Cup Winners Cup in 1971 when The Blues thumped thirteen goals past Luxembourg side Jeunesse Hautcharage without reply winning the tie 21-0 on aggregate which is still an official joint UEFA record.

In the league Chelsea's record victory was a 9-2 win over Glossop in 1906 and still stands as the most league goals Chelsea have scored in a game. This was the game that saw George "Gatling Gun" Hilsdon mark his debut with five goals.

Although not matched, in 2009-10 season Chelsea scored seven goals three times in the season including pressure wins against Aston Villa and Stoke. These helped Chelsea secure their third Premier League title in style under the guidance of Carlo Ancelotti.

However the same season The Blues also secured their biggest ever Premier League win against Wigan, and biggest league margin of victory. Two goals from Nicholas Anelka and a Didier Drogba hat-trick meant that Chelsea secured the title in style with the 8-0 result. This feat was matched in December 2012 when Aston Villa were taken apart at Stamford Bridge for the same score line.

57 FROM EUROPEAN GLORY TO RELEGATION IN FOUR YEARS

After being one of the most successful and exciting teams in the mid to late 1960's the young team that had developed and delivered success in the FA Cup and European Cup Winners Cup at the start of the 1970's.

The European Cup Winners Cup win was the zenith of this great team that featured iconic names such as Peter Bonetti, Charlie Cooke, Peter Osgood and Ron Harris.

The following season Chelsea reached the League Cup Final but decline had started to set in with manager Dave Sexton having problems managing the team and coming to blows with key players such as Peter Osgood and Alan Hudson, which led to them both leaving the club.

As the team that had brought so much success slowly broke up results started to suffer on and off the pitch, extensive developments to Stamford Bridge were being made but they were running late and over budget, putting the club into debt.

With friction inside the club and no money to bring in players to replace quality they had lost the club was relegated from the First Division just four years after lifting the UEFA Cup Winners Cup.

YOUNGEST
CAPTAIN

Ray Wilkins has had many different jobs at Chelsea including Assistant Manager under four different managers, however he started off his association as a player in the youth team.

Wilkins was made Chelsea captain aged just 18 and he was handed the captains armband as manager Eddie McCreadie tried to blend youth players with the surviving veterans of the success at the beginning of the decade.

He took over the captaincy in the summer of 1975 with Chelsea then in the Second Division following relegation the previous season. He was one of the stars of a team that gained promotion to the First Division during the 1976-1977 season.

His performances gained national attention with Don Revie calling him up to the England squad in 1976.

When a lack of investment meant Chelsea were relegated in 1979 Wilkins was sold to Manchester United after making nearly 200 appearances for Chelsea earning two "Player Of The Year awards". He went on to play for Milan, Paris St Germain and Glasgow Rangers before finishing his career in the English lower leagues. His brother Graham also played for Chelsea.

RON HARRIS'S ALL TIME APPEARANCE RECORD

In 1980 Chelsea stalwart Ron Harris brought to an end a long and successful Chelsea career that spanned 19 years. Starting at the club 17 he was part of the team that won the FA Youth Cup in 1961 making his debut in 1962.

Nicknamed "Chopper" due to his reputation as a tough defender known to make crunching tackles in an era where referees were more lenient and tackles were often quite ferocious.

He broke into the first team as Chelsea won promotion back to the First Division in 1963 and became part of the backbone of a team that became one of the most fashionable sides in the country with Chelsea earning a rock 'n' roll reputation for entertaining on and off the pitch.

Harris became Chelsea captain in the mid 1960's leading the club to significant success leading the team out for four major finals, lifting the FA Cup and European Cup Winners Cup trophies in the process.

His career was one of ups and downs as he was a part of the clubs growth in the 1960's and then decline in the wake of financial problems in the mid to late 1970's.

The club were relegated in 1975 and Ron Harris was stripped of the captaincy although he was still a key part of the team, the team bounced back in 1977 but were relegated in Harris's penultimate season as Chelsea started the 1980's in the second tier.

His longevity saw him make a staggering 795 first team appearances a feat that makes him the club's record appearance maker by a considerable distance.

After leaving Chelsea he went on to play six miles down the road at Brentford as player coach.

FIRST
EUROPEAN TROPHY

Winning the FA Cup meant more than the glory of winning a trophy; it saw Chelsea qualify for the UEFA Cup Winners Cup for the first time, entering the contest during the 1970/1971 season.

The UEFA Cup Winners Cup was for European sides that had won their national equivalent of the FA Cup and the format of the competition was a two-legged knockout for each round leading to the final.

The teams involved included world famous clubs such as Real Madrid, and PSV Eindhoven as well as minnows like Finnish side FC Haka.

In the early stages Chelsea overcame Greek side Aris Thessaloniki, CSKA Sofia from Romania and Belgian side Club Brugge without any major scares to reach the semi-final. This saw them pitted against fellow English team Manchester City. This was rare as normally only one team per country was entered; however Manchester City had qualified as holders.

The first leg was at Stamford Bridge and a solitary goal from South African Derek Smethurst just after half time gave Chelsea a slender first leg advantage.

The second leg was another tight affair with a first half own goal from Manchester City goalkeeper Ron Healey giving Chelsea a cushion that they would hold to secure a place in their first European Final.

The Final was in Greece and thousands of Chelsea fans made the trip to Athens. Chelsea took the lead through Peter Osgood in the 56th minute but Madrid managed to scramble a last minute equaliser. With extra time yielding no more goals as with the year before

Chelsea would need a replay to settle a major cup final.

This meant that many travelling fans had to travel home, however a hardy few without accommodation slept wherever they could, including the street, in hope of seeing Chelsea lift the trophy.

The replay was just two days later in the same stadium with each side making just one change to their team sheet.

Chelsea took a two-goal lead into half time courtesy of goals from Peter Osgood and John Dempsey.
Real Madrid did pull one back but Chelsea held on to win the club's first European trophy.

FAMOUS
'BLUE IS THE COLOUR'
SONG HITS THE CHARTS

To celebrate reaching the 1972 League Cup final the club decided to make a song called 'Blue Is The Colour' to commemorate the occasion.

With the playing squad lending their voices to the recording it quickly became a fans favourite.

The song has even been copied by sporting clubs such as a Canadian American football team the Saskatchewan Roughriders. Even the Danish national Olympic football team used it as the official supporters song for the 1972 Summer Olympics.

Before the final the single reached the top 10 in the music charts peaking at no.5 and has been played at Stamford Bridge and at major finals ever since.

The players involved in the recording included Chelsea legends Peter Osgood, Ron Harris and Peter Bonetti - part of a tradition of players singing in football club songs released in the build up to major finals.

In recent times the song has been adapted by the Vancouver Whitecaps and even Japan League side Montedio Yamagata.

Unfortunately in 1972 the song was not a good luck charm as the Blues lost 2-1 in the final as Stoke lifted the trophy however this took little shine off its popularity.

CHELSEA'S MOST UNSUCCESSFUL MANAGER

Whilst some managers have overseen Chelsea during relegations and lean times the manager that has the worst statistical record did not even manage the club for a whole season.

The worst record is Danny Blanchflower's, who was manager between December 1978 and September 1979.

The former Tottenham Hotspur player had been a coach with Spurs but his appointment as manager at Stamford Bridge, surprised many given his ties to a rival and his lack of managerial experience. His only other experience was in international management for Northern Ireland.

Blanchflower lasted just 32 games of which he won just five to give him a win percentage of just 16%. His time in charge spanned two seasons one of which saw Chelsea relegated from the First Division finishing bottom of the table.

His time in charge was a disaster and he left with his tenure more notable for the departure of Ray Wilkins and Peter Bonetti than his exploits on the pitch.

After leaving Chelsea Blanchflower did not manage another club but chose to work in the media instead.

FOUNDING FAMILY LEAVE STAMFORD BRIDGE AFTER 77 YEARS

The Mears brothers Henry Augustus "Gus" and Joseph founded Chelsea in 1905 and their family owned the club for 77 years through the good times and the bad with the club being passed down through three generations.

The son of the original owner Joseph joined the board in 1931 becoming Chairman in 1940 during a tenure that saw the club become Champions of England. He was also involved in the Football Association, becoming Chairman in 1963 and becoming heavily involved in organising the 1966 World Cup.

He even played a part in helping to recover the Jules Rimet Trophy (the original World Cup) when it was stolen weeks before the final, working with the police to catch the criminal who was attempting to ransom the trophy.

Tragically he died in 1966 just two weeks before the start of the World Cup he had worked so hard to organise. Ownership of the club moved to his son Brian who became Chairman in 1969 and set about his vision of turning Chelsea into an all seated stadium.

Sadly the project failed and Chelsea suffered relegation and strife in his later years at the club with only one stand of his dream being completed.

The last few years of his reign at the club were turbulent and he was forced out as chairman and had to sell the club for just £1.

This marked the end of a 77 year era of the Mears family's association with the club.

BUSINESSMEN BUYS
CHELSEA FOR £1

In the late 1970's and 1980's Chelsea struggled on and off the pitch and by 1982 the club was in dire straits struggling to survive.

In 1982 when the Mears family left the club Chelsea were on the brink of bankruptcy and going out of business. The club was saved by Ken Bates, a ruthless and ambitious businessman. He bought the club for just the symbolic fee of £1 taking on the club's deep debts determined to turn things around.

Over the next fifteen years he restructured the club, wrestled back control of Stamford Bridge from development and transformed Stamford Bridge into a modern all-seated stadium.

Bates built the Chelsea Village attached to the ground that featured bars/restaurants and even a hotel. He was a controversial character who was loved and loathed by Chelsea fans at the same time. In the 1990's he clashed with lifelong fan and director Matthew Harding over their visions for the club, a feud that was bitter and drawn out and only ended when Harding died in a helicopter accident in 1996.

Even after leaving his legacy with Chelsea fans was mixed with a blend of respect for what he had done for the club with a dislike for his abrasive style.

Bates left Chelsea soon after Roman Abramovich bought the club in 2003 and stayed true to character by leaving under a cloud.

LOWEST EBB AS CHELSEA ALMOST PLUMMET TO THIRD DIVISION

Since election to the Football League in 1905 Chelsea have bounced between the top two divisions but never dropped below the second tier of English Football.

The closest that The Blues came to relegation to the third tier was in the 1982/1983 season when the club was almost relegated after a terribly inconsistent season that yielded just 11 victories.

The league table was tight and with just two games to go there were around 10 sides that could have been dragged into the dogfight.

In the penultimate game of the season Chelsea travelled to Burnden Park to play Bolton just one point outside of the relegation places and winless in nine games.

The game was a tense one and the game looked like it was going to end in a 0-0 stalemate that helped neither side, however Clive Walker etched himself into Chelsea folklore by lashing home a shot from outside of the penalty area to secure what is now heralded as one of the most important victories in the club's history.

With the league so tightly packed this win saw Chelsea leapfrog Bolton jumping all the way to 14th in the table and a draw in the final game saw Chelsea finish 17th just two points ahead of the relegation places.

ELECTRIC FENCES
TO KEEP THE FANS
OFF THE PITCH

In the 1980's hooliganism was a huge problem in English football affecting games at every level of the professional game.

Football clubs and the government struggled to prevent crowd trouble at games with so called fans using football as an excuse to fight each other.

Chelsea was no exception with Chelsea having its own "firm" known for fighting with fans from rival clubs. Stamford Bridge was often a hostile place with intense fan rivalries reaching fever pitch before, during and after games.

In 1985 with other measures failing and increasing hostility at Stamford Bridge owner Ken Bates resorted to an extreme measure by installing electric fences around the ground to prevent fans from getting onto the pitch during games.

Their introduction was met with outcry by fans and politicians alike with many feeling that the fences were "inhumane".

Chelsea fans however would never experience the "electric" atmosphere of Stamford Bridge as local politicians from the Greater London Council successfully fought to stop them being turned on and eventually the fences were removed altogether without ever being used.

Over time ground regulations, improved policing and a cultural change led to a huge reduction in hooliganism and the modern family friendly is almost unrecognisable in its modern form having had three stands rebuilt and turned into an all seated stadium.

PAUL CANOVILLE BREAKS
THE RACE BARRIER

In January 1985 Paul Canoville scored the fastest second half goal in the history of Chelsea Football Club after 11 seconds in a thrilling 4-4 draw.

However Canoville has a more important role to play in the history of Chelsea Football Club for a different reason that harks back to a dark period in football history.

Three years before the Sheffield Wednesday thriller Paul Canoville made his debut and became the first black player to play for Chelsea.

During his debut as a late substitute for fan favourite Clive Walker against Crystal Palace he was greeted with a chorus of hatred from his own fans because of the colour of his skin.

Despite this abuse he refused to bow to the mob mentality and went on to play over 100 games over five years for Chelsea.

Despite not making the most of his talent he blazed a trail breaking an important barrier in the history of Chelsea Football Club paving the way for future gifted black players to make their way in football.

His career was ended prematurely due to injury but the impact that he had will have a positive impact on Chelsea Football Club for generations to come.

The abuse that he faced is now unthinkable, with Chelsea employing talent from across the world and he was a pioneer that helped changed football for the better.

THE
FORGOTTEN TROPHIES

The 1980's were turbulent times for Chelsea but there was some silverware as the club won the Full Members Cup in 1986 and then again in 1990.

In 1985 English clubs were banned from Europe following the Heysel disaster that saw 39 fans die in the European Cup Final between Liverpool and Juventus. This led to the creation of the Full Members Cup for clubs in the top two divisions of English football as an additional competition to be contested.

The inaugural season of the trophy was the 1985/1986 season and Chelsea were the first winners of the trophy winning a 5-4 thriller against Manchester City at Wembley.

This was a rare bright spot for Chelsea who were a mediocre to struggling First Division side that had not won a trophy in fifteen years.

Chelsea went on to win the trophy again in 1990 this time beating Middlesborough 1-0 in the Final courtesy of a Tony Dorigo goal.

The Full Members Cup was cancelled after seven seasons with the founding of the Premier League and will be remembered as a minor competition barely registering on the honours boards of those that have won it.

It was however a bright spot in a difficult decade for the Blues.

LAST TIME IN
THE SECOND DIVISION

FACT**69**

Chelsea spent six years of the eighties in the Second Division. Having got back into the First Division however, in 1988 The Blues were relegated again to the Second Division.

But Chelsea romped to promotion at the first time of asking. Things did not start well though as they failed to win any of their first six home games.

Things improved and the Blues steadily climbed the table hitting the top in mid December in a few months that saw them see-sawing between the top two places.

They hit a rich vein of form and went 27 league games without defeat including a run of eight victories in a row that pulled The Blues away from their rivals and romp to promotion as Champions by a whopping 17 points.

The star of the side was Kerry Dixon who scored 25 league goals as Chelsea racked up 96 goals.

Finishing with three victories Chelsea reached 99 points which is the club record for the most points ever gained in a single season. This phenomenal feat saw 29 wins, 12 draws and just five defeats.

Chelsea carried on this great form to the First Division finishing fifth in their first season back. Chelsea have not returned to the Second Division since.

FANS OWN THE
PITCH & CLUB NAME

Chelsea Football Club is unique in that the ground and the name Chelsea FC are owned by the fans.

In the late 1970's and 1980's the club struggled due to debts from attempts to renovate Stamford Bridge and a change in ownership ultimately led to the ground being sold to a property development company who could have sold the it and left Chelsea homeless.

When owner Ken Bates wrestled control of the ground back in 1992 when the company that owned Stamford Bridge went bankrupt he came up with a scheme to help secure the long-term future of the club.

He set up and sold Stamford Bridge and the name to a new fan owned company called the Chelsea Pitch Owners. Fans were encouraged to buy shares at £100 each limited to 100 per person to ensure that no one person or organisation could gain control of the organisation.

Each fan could then vote on the future of the organisation in the knowledge that they were helping protect the future of the club.

Roman Abramovich has tried to buy out this group in the past with the aim of moving to a new location but the first vote in October 2011 failed to get enough votes to allow the sale.

CHEERING AN OPPOSITION PLAYER AT WEMBLEY

It is rare for football fans to cheer a player on the opposing side, particularly when their side is playing to reach their first FA Cup Final in 24 years.

In 1994 Chelsea faced Luton in the FA Cup Semi Final at Wembley and the club's second highest goal scorer at the time was playing for the opposition.

Therefore when his name was read out during the line ups he got a rapturous reception from both sets of fans.

Prior to his time at Luton striker Dixon had spent nine hugely successful seasons at Chelsea scoring 193 goals, which makes him the third highest goals in Chelsea history.

A hero to many fans he received a brilliant reaction throughout the game with Chelsea fans repeatedly singing tribute to Luton's centre forward who was serenaded with regular chants of "there's only "One Kerry Dixon".

In the twilight of his career he was unable to have a significant impact on the result.

Chelsea won the semi final 2-0 however in the final minutes of the game with victory seemingly assured it was Dixon's name that rang out across Wembley as the Chelsea faithful paid tribute to one of the most prolific strikers in the club's history.

KINGS
OF WEMBLEY

Chelsea's overall record at Wembley is fantastic with 19 wins between the first appearance a FA Cup Final defeat in 1967 and the 25th a FA Cup Semi Final defeat against Manchester City.

This has seen the club compete at Wembley for the FA Cup, League Cup, Full Members Cup and the Community Shield.

Chelsea were the last team to win the FA Cup at the old Wembley before its reconstruction and the first to win it at the "New Wembley" in 2007. Appearances at the home of football were sporadic between that first appearance in 1967 and the early 90's.

After defeat against Manchester United in the 1994 FA Cup Final Chelsea turned Wembley Stadium from a place of defeat to a fortress, home of many Chelsea triumphs.

Chelsea went on to win the FA Cup at Wembley in 1997 and from that point on it became like a second home making an average of more than one appearance a year. Between 1997 and 2013 Chelsea made 18 appearances, losing just 3 games (excluding penalty shoot-out defeats in the Community Shield).

FACT 73
PLAYING IN THE SNOW

Battling the weather is part of football and throughout the club's history only a handful of games have been called off with the reasons including blanket fog, frozen pitches and power failure.

In 1997 Chelsea travelled inside the Arctic Circle to play Norwegian side Tromso in a European Cup Winners Cup game that Chelsea fans to this day argue should have been called off before kickoff.

The game was played in mid October and due to Tromso's proximity to the North Pole winter had already set in with snow falling heavily in the hours before the game.

With the snow largely cleared before kick off the game started without a hitch. However as the match continued the intensity of the snow increased.

Tromso were two goals up within twenty minutes as snow continued to fall during the game at such a rate that the game had to be stopped twice to clear the snow from the lines on the pitch.

To the frustration of Chelsea manager Ruud Gullit the referee though refused to stop the play and by the time Vialli pulled one back with five minutes to play the pitch was barely visible from the stands.

Tromso scored again before Vialli responded with another goal at the death to give Chelsea two away goals that could have proven vital.

On the return leg the weather was nowhere as bad with the teams playing on grass. With a return to conditions they were accustomed to Chelsea began to overwhelm their opposition.

Chelsea romped to a 7-1 victory with the home fans taunting the hardy travelling fans reminding them of the crazy conditions in the first leg with renditions of "what's it like to play on grass?"

FANCY DRESS
FOOTBALL

The early 90's Chelsea fans started a tradition involving flat caps, curly wigs, Hawaiian shirts and sharp suits.

Injecting some fun into watching their club's final away game of the season Chelsea fans have taken to wearing fancy dress in the stands.

With the last game usually in May the weather is warm enough for a wide range of costumes suitable for a party atmosphere.

For example in 1991 this constituted Beachwear such as surf shorts and Hawaiian shirts at Villa Park, in 1992 this was moustaches and curly wigs to copy a comic TV character with the intention to poke fun at the home supporters at Goodison Park.

The trend of paying homage/mocking the home supporters continued with Sheffield United at Bramall Lane in 1993, this time sporting flat caps of the style traditionally associated with working men in the city. Whereas in 1994 the theme was the Blues Brothers as both Chelsea and the opposition's club colours are blue.

The tradition continues today with pockets of fans still looking forward to the last day of the season and an opportunity to celebrate the last away game with a few thousand friends.

THE HOLLYWOOD
FOOTBALLER

With most footballers retiring in their thirties, before the advent of the Premier League it was common place for players to have a second career after retiring, regardless of the success they may have had on the field.

Peter Osgood famously ran a pub whereas the profession of others varies greatly. Some former players became bricklayers, others going into the media surrounding football, becoming commentators or football writers.

After playing for Wimbledon, Leeds, Chelsea, Sheffield United and Queens Park Rangers Vinnie Jones had loftier aspirations.

Famous for being a hard man on the pitch he had a reputation for hard tackling often taking things too far. In one game for Chelsea he was booked after just three seconds for a foul on a member of the opposition team.

Jones played up to his hard man reputation off the pitch landing a role in *Lock Stock & Two Smoking Barrels* whilst still plying his trade as a professional footballer.

Typecast as a gangster or hired muscle in many of his films he hit Hollywood when he had major roles in *Swordfish* and *Gone in 60 Seconds* acting alongside huge names such as Angelina Jolie, Halle Berry, John Travolta, Nicholas Cage and Hugh Jackman.

FIRST SACKING IN THE PREMIER LEAGUE BRINGS BACK FAMILIAR FACE

In February 1993 after a reasonable start to the season a poor run of results in January and early February saw manager Ian Porterfield sacked.

He earned the unfortunate honour of being the first Premier League manager to be sacked.

With only a few months of the season left Chelsea turned to former playing hero David Webb to take over as caretaker manager.

Webb was a hero to Chelsea fans winning the player of the year award twice and scoring the winning goal in the 1970 FA Cup Final.

As a manager Webb brought stability to a team that had not won in the league for two months, although he lost his first game in charge the second brought victory over local rivals Arsenal that meant fans instantly warmed to Webb the manager.

A run of seven games unbeaten meant ensured that the rot had been stopped with Webb guiding Chelsea to an eleventh placed finish in the league.

Despite this, at the end of the spell his contract was not renewed with the board opting to appoint a more modern manager.

Webb left the club with his status as a Chelsea legend both on and off the pitch intact.

THE ERA OF
THE PLAYER MANAGERS

In 1993 Chelsea appointed a player manager for the first time since John Tait Robertson 88 years previously.

The appointment of Glen Hoddle started a trend of three successive player managers to take the helm.

Hoddle managed Chelsea for three seasons playing in the first two, making 39 appearances and scoring one goal. He introduced a new brand of football, making it to the FA Cup Final in his first season and qualifying for Europe.

Hoddle left to become England manager. His legacy was the players that he signed including Dutch midfielder Ruud Guillit who replaced him.

Guillit was the catalyst for a clutch of high profile names to arrive at the club with Gianfranco Zola, Gianluca Vialli and Roberto Di Matteo amongst them.

He made the perfect start winning the FA Cup in his first season - the first foreign manager to achieve this feat.

He made 18 appearances as manager and was controversially sacked whilst second in the league due to disagreements with the board over a contract.

He was replaced by Gianluca Vialli who inherited a team already in two cup quarter finals and he continued the fine work started by Guillit, winning the League Cup and UEFA European Cup Winners Cup and guiding the team to a fourth in the Premier League that meant qualification for the Champions League.

The last of three player managers, Vialli was sacked five games into the 2000/2001 season despite having won the FA Cup that summer following disagreements with key players.

These three managers gradually evolved the football at Stamford Bridge laying foundations for a further decade of success.

GIANFRANCO
FACT 78   THE GREATEST EVER?

Arguably the club's greatest player is Gianfranco Zola who played for the club between 1996 and 2003 making 312 appearances.

This claim can be verified by a fan vote organised by the club in 2003 that selected the Italian forward. Having achieved personal and team trophies whilst at the club he is a fine candidate for the honour.

Signed from Parma in November 1996 part way through the season, he made an instant impact making many man of the match performances and scoring some sublime goals, one of which led to Manchester United manager Alex Ferguson calling him a "clever little so and so."

His first season saw Chelsea lift the FA Cup with Zola contributing four goals to the cause including an iconic goal against Wimbledon and a trademark 25-yard curler against Liverpool.

That season saw him win the Football Writers Association player of the year award, becoming the first player to do so without playing the whole season. He was also the first Chelsea player to win the accolade.

Zola went on to win the League Cup (1998) FA Cup (1997, 2000) the UEFA Cup Winners Cup and UEFA Super Cup for the team as well as a clutch of individual honours that included being the Chelsea Player of the Year twice (1997, 2003) and a place in the club's centenary XI.

Zola left Chelsea in the summer of 2003 with the club struggling to afford a new deal, when Roman Abramovich arrived just days later he desperately tried to get Zola to stay. But he had already given his word to his old club Caligari that he would sign for them and nothing could convince a gentleman and man of his word such as Zola to change his mind.

CELEBRITY
FANS

With a central London location and a large fan base Chelsea have always had their share of celebrity fans and is not uncommon for fans to rub shoulders with famous names on their way in and out of Stamford Bridge on match days.

With the English game now attracting a global audience these celebrities often attract worldwide fame including Hollywood actors such as Will Ferrell who has been photographed wearing a replica Chelsea shirt on several occasions.

This stretches to the music industry as well with Damon Albarn, Jimmy Page, Lil Wayne all reported to be Chelsea fans.

In the sports world Lord Sebastian Coe the organiser of the London 2012 Olympics is a huge Chelsea fan and he is one of a few Olympic gold medal winning sports personalities to support the club including NBA player Kevin Garnett.

Another high profile fan and the one most involved with the club was Director Lord Richard Attenborough who was involved in the running of the club as far back as 1966 as Vice President and was appointed "Life President of The Club" in 2008. He died aged 90 in 2014.

THE
FAN DIRECTOR

The North Stand of Stamford Bridge is called the "Matthew Harding Stand" in honour of former director Matthew Harding who tragically died in a helicopter crash in 1996 when serving as the club's Vice Chairman.

A lifelong Chelsea fan, Harding was one of the richest men in Britain but preferred to sit in the stands with normal fans than the director's box despite being made part of the board after investing millions into the club.

Matthew Harding and owner Ken Bates did not see eye to eye with the owner worried that Harding was after too much control and may try and buy the club. Harding was seen as "one of us" by the fans whilst Bates was seen somewhat as a pantomime villain as their spat raged both privately and in the press.

He died on his way back from a League Cup defeat against Bolton which left Chelsea fans shell-shocked.

Harding's money was invested in players and in building a new North Stand which was to be named after him just days after his death.

The next game against Tottenham Hotspur was just a few days after his death and whilst Chelsea fans mourned a loss of a family member our normally fierce rivals showed respect to a man that most football fans seemed to be able to identify with.

It is a tribute to his influence that his name is still sung at Stamford Bridge in remembrance.

81 TURNING POINTS IN 4-2 VICTORY OVER LIVERPOOL

One of Chelsea's greatest FA Cup runs nearly ended before it had begun as Chelsea went 2-0 down at half time in the fourth round of the FA Cup in January 1997.

Chelsea faced top of the table Liverpool at Stamford Bridge with the pain of a 5-1 defeat at Anfield fresh in the memory of the players and fans.

Liverpool came blistering out of the blocks to take their half time lead courtesy of goals from Robbie Fowler and Steve McManaman. Things could have been worse for Chelsea with both goal scorers spurning gilt-edged chances to end the tie.

At half time Chelsea changed the game by bringing on Mark Hughes and set about getting back into the match and turning the tie around.

Mark Hughes pulled the first goal back just five minutes into the second half and Gianfranco Zola equalised with a beautiful long-range shot that curled into the right hand side of the net.

It was then the turn of future manager Gianluca Vialli to take control of the game giving Chelsea the lead after 62 minutes, converting a Dan Petrescu through ball. Then with 15 minutes to play Petrescu sealed the game with a bullet header from a Gianfranco Zola free kick.

The game ended 4-2 and from the despair at half time Chelsea had secured a historic victory that would prove key in a season that would lead to glory.

43 SECONDS
TO HEAVEN

One of the quickest goals scored by Chelsea is also one of the most important in the clubs history.

Having reached the FA Cup Final in 1997 it took just 43 seconds for Roberto Di Matteo to put Chelsea into the lead in what was at the time the quickest goal in a final in the history of the competition.

Chelsea faced Middlesbrough on a sunny Saturday in May and the game started with Middlesbrough attacking down to the right but this was broken up and Dennis Wise fed Roberto Di Matteo in the middle of the pitch deep in his own half.

Di Matteo drove forward through the middle of the pitch and about 35 yards from goal he launched a shot that went over the keeper and dipped under the bar to send Chelsea fans into delirium.

Chelsea went on to lift the trophy with Eddie Newton scoring the second goal as The Blues won 2-0 to secure the club's first trophy in 27 years.

As for the quickest FA Cup Final goal his record stood until 2009 when Louis Saha scored for Manchester United against Chelsea after just 25 seconds.

FEWEST DRAWS
IN A SEASON

Chelsea hold the record for the fewest draws in a Premier League season.

In the 1997/1998 season under the management of Ruud Guillit and from February, Gianluca Vialli.

During the season Chelsea drew just three league games in a season and finished fourth, having won twenty games and lost 15 during an up and down season that included a run of four defeats in a row in a terrible period in February.

The draws came away against champions Manchester United in September and at home to Leeds and Wimbledon in December. Chelsea did not draw another game after the

New Year in a phenomenal run of games where they avoided sharing the points.

The Leeds draw was one of the highlights of the season for its robust nature rather than entertainment in a 0-0 draw.

The game was a feisty one with plenty of crunching tackles and tension between the sets of players. This boiled over and Leeds had two players sent off but were able to hang on to claim a point with just 8 outfield players.

THE MOST UNUSED SUBSTITUTE

Since the first substitution in 1965 there have been many important substitutes for Chelsea and fabulous personal performances.

These include a hat trick in March 2004 from Jimmy Floyd Hasselbaink against Wolves to super sub Mikael Forrsell who scored in four games in a row from the bench.

The player with the most substitute appearances for Chelsea is Salomon Kalou who came off the bench 120 times in a six-year career at Stamford Bridge.

The king of the Stamford Bridge substitute's bench was Kevin Hitchcock who warmed the bench more than 244 times a club record. As a goalkeeper he would only be called upon if there was an injury, meaning that he made only 4 appearances from the bench.

Hitchcock joined Chelsea from Mansfield in 1988 and between signing and making his final appearance at the club in 1999 he was affected by injury that prevented him from ever securing the no.1 position, finding himself as a back up to a succession of goal keepers including Dmitri Kharine and Ed De Goey.

Although his last appearance was in 1999 he was at the club until 2001 when he left to join Watford as a goalkeeping coach.

FACT 85

FIRST
FOREIGN XI

It took Chelsea 86 years to progress from Nils Middleboe becoming the first foreign player to play for the club in 1913 to fielding an entirely non-British starting XI .

On Boxing Day 1999 Gianluca Vialli made history as the first manager in English football to name an entirely non-British starting XI, it was a landmark that sparked great debate in football.

By naming four English born substitutes Gianluca Vialli did not name an entirely foreign squad leaving Arsene Wenger to earn the infamous tag of being the first manager to name an entirely foreign squad in February 2005.

The Boxing Day line up featured nine different nationalities from three different continents.

Each player was an international and there were two French World Cup winners Franck Leboeuf and Didier Deschamps.

There was also a future Chelsea manager in the squad that day with Roberto Di Matteo one of two Italian's to feature in this landmark side, the other being Gabrielle Ambrosetti.

The other nationalities to be represented were the Netherlands, Romania, Brazil, Nigeria, Spain, Uruguay and Norway.

THE
PERFECT MANAGER

86

The manager's role at Chelsea can be a poisoned chalice with the demand for results and strained relationships with the club's hierarchy plaguing managers throughout the club's history.

One man who can claim to have a 100% winning record in charge of the Blues is former assistant manager Ray Wilkins who had two spells in temporary charge of the Blues.

The first saw him share responsibility with Graham Rix and record one win and one draw as Gianluca Vialli departed and Claudio Ranieri took over.

The second saw him take charge for one game against Watford in the FA Cup in between Felipe Scolari being sacked and Guus Hiddink taking charge. Chelsea won meaning Ray Wilkins had a 100% record in his second spell.

Chelsea went on to win the FA Cup that season meaning that Wilkins can also claim his part in this triumph both as a manager and later as an assistant manager.

THE POSITION
NAMED AFTER A PLAYER

Few players have had such an impact on the game that they can claim to have had a position on the pitch named after them.

Claude Makélélé can as he defined the modern defensive midfield position during his time at Real Madrid and Chelsea.

Makélélé joined Chelsea in 2003 from Madrid where his manager described him as an average footballer but his team mates said he was irreplaceable. Zinedine Zidane commented that adding to the Los Galacticos was pointless when selling Makélélé, as he was the engine.

Costing £16.8m he was the midfield rock who rarely ventured past the halfway line as he controlled the midfield and set a platform for Chelsea to move the ball forward.

He was a key player in the club's first Championship in 50 years scoring his first goal in the last game of the season. With the last game pointless Chelsea were awarded a penalty and Makélélé was put forward to have the chance to score his first goal for the club.

He stepped up and his first effort was saved, yet somehow he managed to stab the ball home. His only other goal was a stunning curling volley to give Chelsea the lead against Tottenham.

Makélélé left Chelsea aged 35 in 2008 heading for Paris St Germain.

RUSSIAN BILLIONAIRE BUYS CHELSEA AFTER ALMOST BUYING SPURS

In June 2003 owner Ken Bates had taken Chelsea full circle. The club's fortunes on the pitch were the best they had been in years but the financial strife that led to his arrival had returned.

The club owed more than £80m and the debt was becoming unsustainable. The investment in the hotel and other facilities at Stamford Bridge had contributed to the problems.

Unbeknownst to the then current owners, Roman Abramovich was interested in buying a football club. He looked at the available clubs and the final choice was between Chelsea and Tottenham Hotspur.

Fortunately for Chelsea he thought the club was a more attractive buy and completed a deal with Ken Bates, with the former owner becoming chairman.

Abramovich was virtually unknown to football fans but it soon became clear that he was determined to see the club compete at the top of world football, bankrolling it with his personal fortune.

With the club's debts wiped out and money available to spend there was optimism and wild excitement as the newfound wealth saw the club linked to every top player in the world.

The next few weeks saw Chelsea spend a fortune on high profile players including such as Juan Sebastian Veron, Adrian Mutu, Hernan Crespo, Claude Makélélé, Damien Duff and Joe Cole.

Some would be more successful than others but football was changed forever and the era of the super rich owner had been born with Chelsea the pioneers.

In the next decade Chelsea went on to win nearly every available trophy at least once.

THE ARRIVAL OF THE SPECIAL ONE

During the first year under the ownership of Roman Abramovich manager Claudio Ranieri was in his fourth season but with expectations on the increase he was under pressure to mould the new signings into the team quickly and win his first silverware.

Rumours grew that he was going to be replaced at the end of the season, which ratcheted up pressure. When the season finished with Chelsea trophy less he was sacked.

He was replaced by Jose Mourinho who had just won the Champions League with Porto. He walked into his first press conference and made the following statement:

"Please don't call me arrogant I am a European Champion I am not one of the bottle, I think I am a Special One."

This immediately got the attention of the world's media in his first press conference and earned himself the nickname "The Special One."

He spent a considerable amount of money bringing in

new players including those from his former club including Paulo Ferreria, Ricardo Carvalho and Tiago.

He won two trophies in his first season including the Premier League, winning it again in his second season to encase him as a Chelsea hero. The following season Chelsea finished second in the league winning the FA Cup and League Cup.

As time went on his relationship with owner Roman Abramovich became strained particularly with the arrival of Andriy Shevchenko that was reportedly the choice of the owner and not the manager.

At the start of the 2007 things came to a head and early into the new season Mourinho and Chelsea parted company by mutual consent.

Chelsea fans were devastated and the winning attitude that Mourinho instilled at the club and the players he moulded would be a key part of the team for years to come. As we know the Special One would be back.

TEAM OF
THE CENTURY

The year 2005 was special to Chelsea in many ways and marked the club's 100th anniversary.

To commemorate this the club looked back on the players that had played their part in the club's history and let the fans vote for a team that represented the best team over the last 100 years.

The team featured players across many generations but heavily featured those from the 1970's late 1990's and the first decade of the new millennium.

The team saw Peter Bonetti (1960-1979) named as goalkeeper.

In defence the right back was Steve Clarke (1987-1998) with Marcel Desailly (1998-2004) and John Terry named as the central defenders. The final defensive slot went to Graeme Le Saux at left back.

The midfield constituted Charlie Cooke (1966-1978), Dennis Wise (1990-2001) and Frank Lampard.

As Chelsea were playing in a 4-3-3 the link man between the midfielders and the strikers was Gianfranco Zola (1996-2003).

Zola was supporting Peter Osgood (1964-1974) and Bobby Tambling (1959-1970).

THE
RECORD BREAKING SEASON

Jose Mourinho arrived at Chelsea with a big reputation and high expectations as the club entered its centenary season.

He brought in a host of new signings such including Didier Drogba, Arjen Robben, Ricardo Carvalho and Paulo Ferreria. Goalkeeper Petr Cech also joined the club that season but that transfer was agreed the season before.

With such a high profile arrival he was under pressure to make a fast start. He did this in a dramatic fashion winning his first four games including a headline opening day victory over Manchester United.

This form continued and it was clear a new force in English football had arrived. He delivered his first trophy at the earliest opportunity winning the League Cup in February. This was a taste of what was to come.

Despite the pressure Chelsea won the league with three games to spare with the league secured courtesy of a 2-0 victory over Bolton at the Reebok on the 30 April 2005 with Frank Lampard scoring a brace.

Chelsea were dominant setting records across the board during the season:

· Fewest goals conceded in a season (15)
· Most wins in a season (29)
· Most consecutive away wins (9)
· Most points in a season (95)

EUROPEAN CUP
SLIPS AWAY

After losing to Liverpool in the Champions League Semi Final in 2005 and 2007, Chelsea finally overcame their rivals in 2008 with a dramatic extra time win and sent The Blues to their first Champions League Final in the club's history against English Champions Manchester United in Moscow.

In a rain-drenched stadium Chelsea went behind from a Christiano Ronaldo bullet header in the 26th minute, but equalised through Frank Lampard just before half time.

There were no more goals in normal time and extra time despite both sides having chances with Didier Drogba and Frank Lampard hitting the woodwork. In the last few minutes there was a fracas involving most of the players during which Drogba slapped Nemanja Vidic and received a red card.

He became only the second player to be sent off in a European Cup final and it had a huge impact on the match as he was not available to take a penalty in the shoot out.

Man United went first and the shootout saw Michael Ballack and Junior Belletti score for Chelsea. With the score at 2-2 Cristiano Ronaldo had his spot kick saved by Petr Cech.

Lampard gave Chelsea the lead on penalties and Ashley Cole scored his effort along with Hargreaves and Nani for Manchester United. Chelsea were one penalty away from winning the Champions League.

With Drogba off, responsibility fell to captain John Terry. His penalty sent the goalkeeper the wrong way but in the wet conditions he slipped sending the ball past the outside of the post.

With the shoot out continuing Chelsea and Manchester United scored their first penalty in sudden death, when Ryan Giggs converted his penalty Nicholas Anelka had to score but having not wanted to take the penalty in the first place his effort was saved and Chelsea lost in the cruellest fashion.

FORTRESS
STAMFORD BRIDGE

Home advantage has always been important in football and between 21 February 2004 and the 26 October 2008 Chelsea turned Stamford Bridge into an impenetrable fortress in the league. A period that saw Chelsea win the league twice and runners up once.

Going unbeaten at home for a season is a rare achievement but Chelsea were to go 86 games unbeaten spanning three and a half seasons creating an incredible English Football record of invincibility.

This record spanned four managers with Claudio Ranieri starting things off following a defeat to Arsenal going the rest of the 2003/2004 season unbeaten.

Then Jose Mourinho arrived and turned Chelsea into a winning machine home and away, he went unbeaten at home during his entire first period at the club. Interim manager Avram Grant continued this fine form as Chelsea finished second in the league.

All good things must come to an end and Luis Felipe Scolari was at the helm when the record run was broken with an uninspiring 1-0 defeat against Liverpool.

Between the managers this gave a share of the record as follows Claudio Ranieri (6 games), Jose Mourinho (60 games), Avram Grant (16 games) and Felipe Scolari (4 games).

WINNING
THE DOMESTIC DOUBLE

In 2010 the battle for the Premier League title with Manchester United went to the wire with Chelsea holding a one-point lead going into the final game.

Both teams were at home and Chelsea knew that victory over Wigan Athletic would secure the club's third Premier League title in Ancelotti's debut season in charge of the club.

The pressure was on Chelsea but it took only six minutes for Nicholas Anelka to give Chelsea the lead and around half an hour into the game Wigan conceded a penalty. After arguments with Didier Drogba over who would take it Frank Lampard converted to put the game out of the reach of a dejected Wigan.

The second half was a massive party with Chelsea scoring six more goals that included a Didier Drogba hat-trick that gave him the golden boot as the club to secured the title with a record league win that has since been match but not beaten.

This was a season that had already seen Chelsea score seven goals on three occasions and Chelsea broke the record for most goals scored in a Premier League season.

The season was not over, a week later Wembley beckoned for an FA Cup Final against Portsmouth.

Courtesy of a Didier Drogba free kick The Blues won the game 1-0 and won the FA Cup/Premier League domestic double for the first time in Chelsea's history.

THE MIRACLE OF
THE NOU CAMP

Chelsea have crossed swords with Barcelona in the Champions League in a series of hotly contested and turbulent fixtures that had more than their share of scandal since 1999.

Barcelona won a semi-final tie in 2009 in controversial circumstances - the Chelsea players were convinced that they should have been awarded a penalty

In 2012 Chelsea met their Catalan rivals once more with Barcelona widely accepted to be the best team in the world and Chelsea the clear underdogs. In the first leg at Stamford Bridge Barcelona appeared more like the home side controlling almost all the possession and creating chances. Just before half time Chelsea scored on the counter attack, defending like Trojans the Blues held on to take a slender 1-0 lead to the second leg at the Nou Camp.

The pressure at the Nou Camp was immense, it was widely expected that Barcelona would win. Especially after scoring twice with John Terry getting sent off for violent conduct all within a few minutes of the first half.

Behind on aggregate and a man down the commentators were convinced it was over. However Chelsea refused to go quietly. Ramires shocked 90,000 Catalans with a sublime chip on the counter attack to give Chelsea the lead on away goals.

Chelsea spent the next 45 minutes constantly defending as Barcelona dominated to re-establish their lead, hitting the post, and world player of the year Messi missing a penalty. In the dying minutes another Barcelona attack was thwarted and lumped clear. Fernando Torres had stayed forward and found himself clear through on goal with no Barcelona player within 20 yards.

He rounded the keeper and scored silencing all but the 500 Chelsea fans in the ground and sending Chelsea to their second Champions League final.

In March 2012 Chelsea sacked manager Andre Villas Boas with the club on a downward spiral, struggling in the league and after defeated 3-1 in the first leg of a Champions League second round tie against highly rated Napoli.

It appeared that Chelsea would end the season without any trophies and outside of the Champions League qualification places.

Andre Villas Boas' former assistant Roberto Di Matteo was appointed caretaker manager setting into motion an extraordinary series of events.

Chelsea stormed back to defeat Napoli in extra time setting up a quarter final against Benfica that saw Raul Meireles finally putting the game out of the reach of Benfica in injury time.

Chelsea faced Barcelona who many called one of the greatest in the history of European football and despite being huge underdogs progressed to a final against Bayern Munich.

Having finished sixth in the league The Blues went into the final knowing that they had to win the competition to ensure they would qualify for the competition the season after.

Chelsea won on penalties to win the Champions League for the first time in the club's history becoming the first team in London to win Europe's most important trophy.

BEATING THE
GERMANS ON PENALTIES

After beating the "best in the world" Chelsea faced four time champions Bayern Munich. The final took place at the Allianz Arena, Bayern's home, a decision made more than a year before the final with Bayern as firm favourites.

A banner in the Bayern end read, "our city, our stadium, our cup" and despite equal allocations the majority of "neutral" tickets seemed to belong to Bayern fans.

Bayern dominated for 80 minutes but could not break through a steadfast Chelsea defence. Then in a moment of seeming inevitability scored with just 8 minutes left. The atmosphere in the stadium was one of victory with 80% of a neutral crowd in Bayern red.

With just two minutes to play Drogba scored a bullet header from a corner to send the tie to extra time. As in the semi-final Chelsea conceded a penalty but Petr Cech saved from former Chelsea player Arjen Robben. With deadlock after 120 minutes the game went to penalties. Juan Mata missed as Bayern raced to a 3-2 lead. Cometh the hour, cometh the goalkeeper and Petr Cech saved his second penalty of the game from Isla Olic. After Ashley Cole levelled Cech got a fingertip to Bastian Schweinsteiger final penalty as it bounced off the post and into the penalty area.

Chelsea were once again one kick from winning the Champions League and up stepped Didier Drogba in what was expected to be his last game for the club.

He took a short run up and rolled the ball into the bottom left hand corner sending Chelsea fans watching across the world crazy.

Chelsea had beaten a German team in their own stadium on penalties to win the Champions League with an interim manager and their star striker scoring the winner. There has never been a better Chelsea script.

FRANK LAMPARD BREAKS BOBBY TAMBLING'S GOAL SCORING RECORD

In the summer of 2001 Chelsea spent a sizeable £11m signing midfielder Frank Lampard from local rivals West Ham. Some fans feared that he wouldn't live up to his transfer fee, but these proved unfounded, as over the next twelve seasons Lampard became one of the most famous and successful footballers in the world, breaking records for both club and country.

On 11 May 2013 Frank Lampard scored his 202nd and 203rd club goals to equal and overtake Bobby Tambling as the club's record goal scorer. A midfielder by trade Lampard was for the best part of his career more prolific than most strikers and he holds the record for most Premier League goals by a midfielder.

His trademarks are arriving late into the penalty area to finish off a move and as a penalty taker. His first two seasons brought 15 goals which is around average for a midfielder but from the 2003/2004 season onwards he became prolific averaging 15 goals or more for the next decade.

Lampard's Landmark Goals
- Brace away against Bolton in April 2005 to secure club's first title in fifty years.
- Scored in Champions League Final defeat to Manchester United in 2008.
- Scored in the FA Cup Final vs. Everton in 2009.

His goals contributed to Chelsea's most successful generation, winning the Premier League three times, the FA Cup four times, the League Cup and community shield twice.

As well as these domestic honours in the absence of John Terry he led Chelsea to victory in the Champions League Final in 2012 and the Europa League Final in 2013.

COMPLETING
THE EUROPEAN SET

In November 2012 Chelsea were knocked out of the Champions League in the stages a place in the Europa League was a small consolation.

Despite a hectic schedule that saw Chelsea play 9 games in just 24 days they made the final where they faced Portuguese side Benfica in Amsterdam. After taking the lead with a trademark Torres goal Chelsea were pegged back and the game looked to be heading into extra time.

However for a second European final in the row it was a Chelsea corner that would result in a game changing goal. In injury time and the scores tied at 1-1 Branislav Ivanovic connected to a corner with a looping header that drifted into the net in front of the delirious Chelsea fans sealing the club's fifth European trophy.

Winning the Europa League meant that Chelsea are the only British team to have won a complete set of European trophies, this set is the Super Cup, Europa League, Cup Winners Cup and the Champions League.

RETURN OF THE
SPECIAL ONE

When Rafael Benitez left Chelsea at the end of his contract the club and its fans were looking for a permanent manager that would be more popular and restore the feeling or harmony within the club.

Since leaving Chelsea in 2007 Jose Mourinho had always spoken of having "unfinished business" at Chelsea and a love for the club.

It was also reported that he had kept in regular contact with owner Roman Abramovich with the two patching up their differences.

During the 2012/2013 season Mourinho was manager at Real Madrid but his relationship with the club and the fans was deteriorating and there was speculation that he would leave the club.

With Real Madrid failing to win the La Liga and Mourinho at war with some key players it was confirmed that he would be leaving the Spanish club at the end of the season. This led to a nervous period as Chelsea fans waiting to see if Mourinho would be in the running for the soon to be vacant managers job at Chelsea.

After months of speculation the club confirmed that Jose Mourinho would be making a dramatic return to Stamford Bridge as manager.

At his first press conference he was calmer and more humble than his first preferring the moniker "The Happy One".

Sources

Chelsea FC – The Official Biography Rick Glanvill
The Chelsea FC Miscellany – Rick Glanvill
Chelsea and English Football in the nineties – Richard Micallef
Chelsea the 100 year history – Brian Mears

The 100 Facts Series

Celtic, *Steve Horton*   978-1-908724-10-6
Chelsea, *Kristian Downer*   978-1-908724-11-3
Liverpool, *Steve Horton*   978-1-908724-13-7
Manchester City, *Steve Horton*   978-1-908724-14-4
Manchester United, *Iain McCartney*   978-1-908724-15-1
Newcastle United, *Steve Horton*   978-1-908724-16-8

ABOUT CHILDLINE

You can contact *ChildLine* about anything - no problem is too big or too small. If you're feeling worried, scared, stressed or just want to talk to someone you can contact *ChildLine*. We're here to offer information and support whenever you need us.

We understand that it can be difficult to trust someone and tell them about what is happening or how you are feeling.

We want to help you feel confident when you use *ChildLine* and show what you can expect from us.

How can I contact *ChildLine*?

Call free on 0800 1111 or visit http://www.childline.org.uk/

www.childlinerocks.co.uk

ChildLine Rocks is an annual charity rock concert organised under the auspices of *ChildLine 20*, an independent committee set up to raise £2,000,000 for *ChildLine* to celebrate 20 years of *ChildLine's* existence.

Lightning Source UK Ltd.
Milton Keynes UK
UKOW06f0141011215

263833UK00001B/3/P